HOME WINE-MAKING
WITHOUT FAILURES

Also by H. E. Bravery

HOME WINE-MAKING ALL THE YEAR ROUND
HOME BREWING WITHOUT FAILURES
THE SIMPLE SCIENCE OF WINE AND BEER MAKING

HOME WINE-MAKING
without failures

H · E · BRAVERY

Foreword by
NOËL WHITCOMB

AVENEL BOOKS · NEW YORK

To
NOËL WHITCOMB
in sincere appreciation

© MCMILVIII, MCMILX H. E. Bravery
This edition published by Avenel Books
a division of Crown Publishers, Inc.
by arrangement with Max Parrish & Co., Ltd.
bcdefghijkl
Manufactured in the United States of America

Contents

1. To Begin With — 1
2. Root Wines — 20
3. Wines from Other Vegetables — 24
4. My Special Recipes — 26
5. Fruit Wines — 44
6. Sherry — 61
7. Dried-fruit Wines — 64
8. Flower and Sugar Wines — 68
9. Mixed Drinks for the Party — 72
10. Cider, Ale, Beer and Stout — 75
11. If You Experiment — 82
12. Wine-making and the Law — 86
13. The Scientific Approach — 88
14. Fruit Wines the Modern Way — 107
15. Grape Wines — 125
16. That Stewed Fruit Flavour — 129

CONTENTS

17. Dried Fruit Wines the Modern Way 144
18. Root Wines the Modern Way 149
19. Champagne and Sparkling Wines 153
20. Sugar, Acid and Alcohol 158
21. Some Questions and Answers 170
22. Grow Your Own Wine 182
23. Growing Soft Fruits 191
24. Growing Tree Fruits 204
25. Growing Grapes 211
26. Monthly Gardening Reminders 215

Index 219

Foreword

It is about four years since I first had the good fortune to receive a letter from Harold Bravery. I remember it well. A thin morning, it was.

In case you do not know what a thin morning is, let me explain. In the life of a newspaper columnist there are two sorts of morning.

There is the morning upon which ideas whizz and dodge round the brainbox like traffic around Piccadilly Circus; all telephones in sight (a columnist's office is like a bookmaker's – all telephones and ashtrays) are ringing at once, with chaps at the other end of the line eagerly describing useful stories; the mail is crammed with pungent, controversial stuff; and the whole problem facing the chap at the typewriter is what to use from this *embarras de richesse* for his column, and what to cast aside.

Then there is the other type of morning: all telephones are silent; the brain is churning like one of those old-fashioned toffee-making machines; not an idea in sight; a space in the paper to fill – and nothing to write about: a thin morning.

It was on such a morning that, in the sparse pile of mail, sandwiched between a chain-letter and a request for a loan of £4 10s., I unhopefully read a typewritten note signed 'H. E. Bravery'.

About wines, it was. Home-made wines. With the automatic, fatalistic reaction of the journalist who finds himself with barely time to write the required number of words before the last moment at which his copy must be ready for type-setting, I began tapping out a column about home-made wines. All Bravery's own work.

I sent a copy-boy up with the manuscript. Then I stuck my hat on and went out for a nourishing half-pint, gloomily reflecting that this was not one of Whitcomb's masterpieces that had just escaped from the typewriter. However, I figured sadly, the readers – generous, kind-hearted lot – would perhaps forgive me for this one. They would understand. In time they might even forget.

Little did I know that I had pressed the button that ignites the main fuse to one of the country's most popular hobbies.

Little did I realise that, the following morning, readers all over the place would be thumping their breakfast tables with a beaming smile and calling to their wives: 'Hey – Mabel – cut this bit out of the paper. At last old Whitcomb has hit on a matter of interest.'

My mail next morning was considerable. If I remember rightly (and don't let me kid you – I *do* remember rightly) there were 20,000 letters. Next day there were 10,000 more. I could hardly have unleashed more passion if I had attacked the Irish.

Everybody wanted to make this splendid wine for a bob a bottle.

They wanted more recipes. So I got them – from Bravery.

Then came the problems. One man complained he had a hole in the ceiling above where his wine bottles had been. 'Don't cork them tightly so soon next time,' I advised him. After I had asked Bravery, of course.

Soon after that, the best mail of all started pouring in. Letters of appreciation from folk who said that, for the first time, their home-made wine was really first-rate.

So many of them were thanking me that, in October 1955, I printed the following under the heading 'Mr. Bravery Deserves a Medal'.

Come Christmas I shall be drinking a toast to Mr Bravery. And so I should.

For there is a bookcase in my office that used to contain books – but now it's stacked like an off-licence with home-made wines from H. E. Bravery.

He's an extraordinary chap, this Bravery. In the home-made guzzling circles of this country, he has done me a bit of good.

You may often hear people say: 'If it is a matter of what is going to win the Cambridgeshire, I would not lean heavily on Whitcomb's opinion. But in the matter of home-made wines – Whitcomb's a winner!'

All because of Bravery. He certainly knows his elder-berries. Not a step do I take in advising chaps who have a hole in the dining-room ceiling through corking their bottles too tightly – without consulting H.E.B.

Thousands of people have written to thank me for the smashing drop of Christmas cheer they have made – for a bob a bottle – from my recipes. All recipes from Bravery.

Yet I've never met him. I don't even know what his initials stand for.

I know now. I have just met him for the first time. Yet more than 100,000 *Daily Mirror* readers have already used either his recipes or his know-how, according to the letters I have received—and goodness knows how many more who have not written.

In this book he has collected the knowledge gained from his own experience together with a valuable cross-section of all the snags that beginners are likely to come up against, and how to avoid them.

Now that I know a fair bit about it myself, I would say that you couldn't find a better book on the subject.

He knows his stuff, does Harold Bravery – and what a good drop of stuff it is!

Good health!

Author's Preface

I hope that this book will be the means by which countless people will derive the pleasure and satisfaction which comes from drinking wines that they have made in their own homes. Those who have failed, or have been disappointed with previous attempts, will find the reasons in this book – and the remedy.

All those who wish they could make strong, delicious crystal-clear wines need wish in vain no longer: they *can* make them, easily, quickly and for a trifling initial outlay. And in order to make each process as easy as possible to understand, I shall deal with each one separately and in detail.

Those with gardens and those within easy reach of wild fruits and flowers are lucky, for they need only four pounds of sugar and threepennyworth of yeast to turn out a gallon of wine almost indistinguishable from commercial products costing fifteen shillings a bottle. For those who have to buy their ingredients the cost is a little more, but rarely more than six shillings a gallon, or about one shilling per ordinary wine bottle.

During the writing of this book I have been asked to help with many hundreds of wine-making problems by people in all parts of this country (and from as far afield as Canada), who had followed misleading directions and recipes and had consequently landed in difficulties. Their inquiries are especially appreciated, for they have helped me enormously in writing a book which tries to answer all the questions.

I would like to thank readers of my wine articles and of the *Daily Mirror* for the recipes they have so kindly sent me. A selection of the best of them is included in this book.

I must also record my sincere thanks to Bob and Meryl Stoner for untold help, and to the Chief Chemist and Manager of a famous British Winery (who wishes to remain anonymous), for valuable advice given over the years. Much of this advice is incorporated in the chapters that follow. H.E.B.

I
To Begin With

If you want to make wine there is no excuse for not doing so: you need neither licence nor cellar and the utensils may already be in your house, flat or caravan – for wine may be made in the smallest of places. To make a couple of gallons of wine is no more bother than to bake a tray of cakes or pickle a few jars of onions, and in comparison the rewards of your labours are far more pleasurable.

A word of warning: The fact that home-made wines do not exceed fourteen per cent (by volume) of alcohol leads the uninitiated to believe that they can drink unlimited quantities without it having effect upon them. How wrong they are! It is a saying in country districts that 'home-made wine is all right when you know how to drink it'. The unsuspected kick in home-made wines has to be felt to be believed. Drink home-made wine as you would drink neat whisky.

Before we begin, I ought to say that two people using the same recipes do not necessarily turn out identical wines any more than they would turn out identical sponge-cakes by using the same mixture. Why? The answer lies, probably, in the fact that one may make a good cup of tea while the other does not, but – tea, sponge-cake or wine – there is always someone to like it the way *you* have made it.

Water and ingredients doubtless have a lot to do with this variation of wines turned out from the same recipe. Fruit and vegetables of different varieties in one brew; harder or softer water in various districts; a wet or dry summer, which would affect the sugar content of fruits; rich or poor soil in which the roots were grown – all these must be allowed for. Commercial producers offset such differences in the quality of their grapes by careful blending, which is a highly skilled operation carried out in laboratories, and which results in each brand of wine containing all the characteristics that have made it popular. Thus two bottles of the same brand of wine will taste identical, even though one bottle may contain as many as eight or nine different wines of varying ages against the other's four or five.

If commercial producers have this advantage over us home producers, do not begrudge them it, for it is the only one they have – as we shall see.

Utensils

The best utensil to use for boiling ingredients and juices is one of good quality enamel; one sold under a proprietary name is most reliable. It must not be chipped.

Cheap enamel utensils often contain lead in the glaze and this might be boiled into the brew; if this happened the wine would be dangerous.

If aluminium or copper is used there is a slight risk of minute particles of the metal being boiled into the brew. This might poison the yeast, and fermentation would not take place.

For fermentation purposes and for soaking fruits and flowers we may use a china vessel or one made of polythene. China vessels should not be too wide at the rim as this exposes too large a surface to the air. A polythene bucket is ideal – but do make sure it is of polythene, as some plastics are not suitable. And choose a pale colour or a white one. Where large batches of wine are made, a polythene dustbin makes an excellent fermentation vessel, as does a strong polythene bag, lining a worn-out barrel or similar vessel.

TO BEGIN WITH

Polythene has the advantage that it is unbreakable. A polythene bucket may be used for all wine-making purposes except boiling the ingredients.

Do not use enamel vessels for fermentation and do not use a galvanized vessel for any part of wine-making.

The Best Ingredients

All *fruits* must be ripe, but not over-ripe. A few shrivelled grapes or blackcurrants are unlikely to harm a brew, but in the case of large fruit such as plums, the doubtful ones should be picked out.

The choice of *roots* (beetroot, parsnips, etc.) for wine-making purposes must not be dismissed so readily. The best, in fact I would say the *only*, roots suitable for wine-making are those that are old and shrivelled. Parsnips that have been stored throughout the winter or left in the soil are at their best for our purpose in March, as are old potatoes bought in June when the new ones are coming in. If they are well shrivelled and sprouting, so much the better. (Rub off the sprouts before using them.) These old roots contain less starch than the fresher ones, and we do not want starch in wines for it slows down the clearing process. Besides this, when old roots are used they flavour the wine less, and it is not in the least bit 'earthy'.

Important Note on Ingredients

It is a mistake to believe that using more ingredients, or less water, or more sugar or yeast, than is prescribed in the recipes, will produce a more potent wine. The strength of wine is decided by the volume of alcohol in which the yeast can live and continue to do its work, and not on the quantity of any ingredients. Too much sugar makes the wine far too sweet. More yeast makes no difference at all, simply because it cannot make more alcohol than it can live in – as we shall see under 'fermentation' (p. 13).

Age makes no difference to the alcohol content of wines. Too many ingredients will produce a liquid of too high a specific gravity – a liquid containing too many solids per ratio of water, in other words a liquid which is too thick – and this will take a very long time to clear.

The rule is, therefore: do not use more ingredients than are prescribed in the recipe.

My recipes are designed to produce approximately one gallon of wine; not two or three quarts according to the extent of evaporation and the formation of lees. It will be noted that many recipes begin with five quarts of water. If this fifth quart were omitted, when the wine had finished fermenting its specific gravity would be high and therefore it would clear more slowly. Less water, then, would have the same effect as using more ingredients in the amount of water stated. Do not forget that fifth quart – or extra pint as the case may be.

STRAINING

Fine muslin is best for straining mixtures produced when making root wines. Tie one piece on the tub – allowing sufficient sag – and place a second piece over this. This top piece containing the solids can be lifted off without letting them fall into the brew.

Jelly bags or similar things made of suitable material are needed for fruit juices, as will be seen in the recipes.

SUGAR AND YEAST

Always use white sugar, and always make certain that all the sugar is dissolved before adding anything – such as wheat and raisins – to the brew. If all the sugar is not dissolved the yeast might not ferment it properly and some of the sugar might settle in the form of syrup and be left in the lees when they are thrown away. The wine might then be quite sharp. With a lot of other stuff in the brew, it is quite impossible to tell whether all the sugar is dissolved or not.

Baker's yeast is all we need bother with at this stage and this can be obtained from your local bakehouse. Yeast is added at the rate of one ounce to one, two or three gallons.

Do not add the yeast too soon as a temperature well below boiling point will destroy the yeast organism and fermentation will not then take place.

Rainwater for Wine-making

Being naturally soft, and 'sweeter' than tap water, rainwater will make far better wines; unfortunately it is heavily contaminated both chemically and micro-biologically. Nevertheless, it can be rendered quite safe by careful filtering and boiling.

If you are sufficiently interested and have the time to take the trouble that a friend of mine goes to you will not regret it.

First he collects the water; then he filters it twice and boils it for fifteen minutes regardless of whether he will be boiling it again when making the wine (as in root-wine making) or whether he will be sulphiting the must when making a fruit wine.

This is how he collects it. He waits until rain has been falling for an hour, so that dust from the roof and gutters has been washed away. He then puts a tub under the fall-pipe and collects about five gallons. This he allows to stand overnight. The clear water is then poured off any solids at the bottom of the vessel, and put into a sawn-off barrel fitted with a tap.

Under this tap is a stone jar which is also fitted with a tap. In the top of the stone jar there is a polythene funnel with a knob of cotton-wool pressed gently into place.

The water from the barrel runs very slowly – hardly more than dripping – through the half-turned-on tap on to the cotton-wool. The partly filtered water runs into the stone jar and out at the bottom into a second jar which also has a funnel fitted with cotton-wool. The partly filtered water runs through this second layer of cotton-wool and into the second jar.

By cleverly arranging the tub on a bench, the first jar on a box and the second jar on the floor, and by carefully regulating the flow – all this taking him about ten minutes – he can leave the water to double-filter itself while he prepares his ingredients.

If the filtering is prepared last thing at night the water is ready for use by the following morning. Admittedly, filtering in this way does take hours, but it does it itself.

Readers wishing to use rainwater must be warned not to use water from a lead roof or from one covered in tarred felt.

THE ENEMIES

The greatest enemies of successful wine-making are acetic bacteria, wild yeast (and bacteria and the spores of fungi which are often present with wild yeast), and pectin. Let me deal with each in turn.

If allowed to contaminate wines, *acetic bacteria* will convert the alcohol into acetic acid, thereby giving the wine a vinegary or very bitter taste. The main cause of acetification – as it is called – is exposure to air. This shows the risk involved in allowing wines to ferment in uncovered or lightly corked bottles.

Wild yeast is always present in the atmosphere; it collects on the skins of fruits as they reach maturity, and with this yeast come harmful bacteria and the spores of certain fungi. To make good wines we must destroy this yeast and the bacteria and fungi spores at the outset, otherwise we might produce a sour wine or one which will not taste like wine at all.

Wild yeast and bacteria will begin fermenting wines that have been bottled for months. Really magnificent wines have been spoiled by the maker thoughtlessly leaving the wines exposed to danger, and if allowed to collect on wines – through the fermenting brew being left uncovered – wild yeast and bacteria will ruin the wine at the outset, but this might not become evident for quite some time.

Wild yeast will begin fermenting fruit-and-water mixtures left for short soaking periods. Many old-fashioned recipes allow for this ferment to make the wine; as will be seen from the foregoing, this method is a very risky one, for it means that wild yeast, the spores of fungi, bacteria – in fact, most of the enemies of wine-making – are with you from the start.

The wild yeast, bacteria and fungi on utensils, etc., will be destroyed during the making of the wines, so these need not worry us. If wild yeast or bacteria reach the wine after it has cleared the wine will go cloudy and be ruined – for there is no cure once the damage has been done.

Wild yeast and bacteria have been known to ruin bottled fruits; they have begun to turn them into sour wines. Even tinned fruits have been known to become 'blown'. All these troubles are caused by wild yeast and the fungi and bacteria which are present with it. The trade goes to great lengths to ensure that wild yeast does not ferment their grape juice. All juices are treated with sulphur dioxide (which is later precipitated) and a specially selected yeast is introduced into the juice for the purpose of fermenting it.

Sulphiting the juices is not recommended to the beginner, but there is nothing to stop us following the methods of the trade in our own way. After all, I cannot imagine the trade letting millions of bottles of wine go sour each season.

Wild yeast must not be confused with natural yeast,

which will often produce quite good wines if allowed to work alone. Unfortunately the natural yeast, which forms the bloom on grapes and other fruits such as plums and gooseberries, is too often accompanied by 'undesirable' strains of yeast and bacteria, which are the cause of most of the troubles so well known to the home winemaker.

As I have already mentioned, the trade sulphite the juices so that these 'undesirable' ferments are held in check while the natural yeast, or a specially prepared yeast culture, is allowed to ferment the juice unhindered.

Most people rely on the greengrocer for their wine ingredients, which, by the time they are received, have passed through markets and shops and been exposed to all sorts of dirt and bacteria. Washing with cold water, or pouring boiling water over them, is of little use; boiling is necessary if the bacteria are to be prevented from harming the wine. As we shall see, boiling the fruits themselves produces wine that will not clear, so we must boil only the strained juice. Plums, gooseberries and other fruit gathered fresh from the garden often produce good wines without the addition of yeast, but I have found that when the natural yeast is allowed to make the wine, 'undesirable' ferments take place at the same time and spoil the wine. We may add tartaric acid, and this will certainly hold 'undesirable' ferments in check, leaving the healthy yeast to ferment alone. Unfortunately, so much tartaric acid has to be used that the resulting wine is usually far too acid. Besides this, when natural yeast is allowed to make the wine the ferment is usually a long-drawn-out and erratic process lasting perhaps several months, which starts and stops at the slightest variation of temperature. The beginner might well cork the wine too soon with the result that the corks blow out or there are a series of explosions.

In any event, a long slow ferment is to be avoided if we are to keep our wines free from the troubles which so often arise from their being left to ferment in an 'open' vessel for months on end.

Frankly, I shall never understand how anyone has ever made wines by leaving the crushed fruit to soak for weeks and then, after the sugar and yeast have been added, allowing it to ferment for several weeks in a tub and then for many more weeks in uncorked or lightly corked bottles. But they have done it, I know they have, and they have never taken precautions against any of the enemies of wine-making. There are thousands of these people throughout the country who for years have made good wines in this way. But then their luck gave out and they gave up wine-making, for their brews went sour or turned to vinegar, would not clear or turned out insipid and flat. And they never bothered to find out why. Let's hope one or two of these people are reading this book.

The short soaking period advised in my recipes is not long enough to allow for the yeast and bacteria to begin their work. The short boiling period is sufficient to give safeguard and at the same time is not long enough to give the juice – and therefore the wine – a 'cooked' flavour. However, should it happen that under exceptional circumstances, a fruit-and-water mixture begins fermenting of its own accord, the reader is advised to strain at once and boil immediately, and then carry on with making the wine.

Pectin is a glutinous or 'sugary' substance present in greater or less degree in all fruit: mainly found in the skin and pips but, in any case, in the fleshy and pithy parts of the fruits themselves. If allowed in wines other than in minute quantities, pectin will hold itself in suspension and produce a permanent cloudiness which I have found quite impossible to clarify.

People have written to me complaining that they had to throw their wine away after waiting years for it to clear.

To get a pectin-free juice, we merely crush the fruit and strain out the juice without applying heat of any kind. Boiling the fruit themselves is the cause of the trouble and even pouring boiling water on certain fruits will give pectin trouble.

As with all things, prevention is better than cure. My recipes are designed to guarantee against an overload of pectin. But the problems of acetic bacteria, other harmful bacteria and wild yeast are not so easily disposed of. It must be remembered that contamination by any of these micro-organisms must be prevented, for there is no cure once the damage has been done.

The Wine Fly

A lot of nonsense is talked about the wine fly. It is true that these tiny flies will sometimes make their appearance where there is wine fermenting, but to say that they alone are responsible for souring of wines is wrong. If the fly can get into the wine then so can air, and it is a safe bet that the bacteria in the air turned the wine long before the fly had had a chance to do any harm. Leaving the wine corked loosely is inviting trouble, of course, and if this were done then the wine fly might very well get in and cause trouble first.

Covering as I have directed will not only prevent the fly from entering but will also prevent to some extent the smell of fermenting wine reaching it and inviting it into the house. I rarely see a wine fly.

Cotton-wool covering filters out any bacteria that may be in the air and this will certainly prevent the wine fly from causing trouble.

Sterilization

If the following precautions seem somewhat tedious, remember that they are the difference between success and failure, and after all, they only take five minutes. Remember, too, that they are no more trouble than your usual precautions for an afternoon's successful fruit bottling.

Knives, graters – in fact all utensils used before the boiling stage – need not be sterilized, since any harmful bacteria on these are automatically destroyed during the process. Straining cloths and fermenting vessels must be sterilized, and this is best done just before the ingredients are ready for straining. Fermenting vessels and straining cloths are harbourers of harmful bacteria, as are chipped and cracked utensils.

Straining cloths are merely boiled for a few minutes. Scald fermenting vessels well, or use sulphur dioxide, about which I shall have something to say later.

So much for the early stages. The next step we must take is to ensure that the brew is kept well covered during the all-important fermentation period. Most of us would cover our brews as a matter of course, but here it is best to use a double thickness of blanketing and a sheet of brown paper, each of which must be tied down tightly. Alternatively – and this might prove more convenient for most people – use a sheet of thin polythene and tie it in place with thin string. This will give excellent protection.

Remember that this is a risky period for fermenting wines and we are taking the best precautions we can to prevent our wines becoming contaminated by wild yeast and bacteria.

As already mentioned, exposure to air is the main cause of all the trouble. On the Continent certain vinegars are produced merely by exposing wine to air for short periods of time.

The wine must be left covered for fourteen days: at this stage fermentation will have slowed down and the time has come to use isinglass, and to put the wine into bottles or stone jars, where fermentation continues.

The saucepan to be used for dissolving the isinglass must be scalded, and while the isinglass is dissolving, the bottles or jars and their corks must be sterilized by boiling them in a pail of water or by baking in an oven. I myself use a five per cent solution of sulphur dioxide (SO_2) and have found this to be the quickest and simplest method of sterilization. Sulphur dioxide is quite safe – it is used extensively by the trade – but the whiff of gas one sometimes gets whilst using it is like that of strong smelling salts.

If you cannot get sulphur dioxide from a chemist, read the last paragraph on page 89. One pint of this home-made solution will sterilize four or five gallon-size jars or a dozen bottles. Pour the solution into the first bottle and swirl it round, then pour into the next bottle and so on. This pint might not be reliable for further use, so throw it away. The rest may be saved for future use. The solution will also rid jars of mustiness and the smell of stale wine.

Having used the solution, rinse the bottles inside with boiled water that has cooled a bit. All this takes only a few minutes, and the slight odour remaining at this stage will not harm the wine in any way.

Stoppers and corks may be immersed in this solution for a few minutes and then dipped in boiled water. There is no need to dry either the bottles or the corks.

When the still fermenting wine is put into stone jars or bottles, the top of each one must be covered with a small piece of polythene, pressed down all round and secured with a strong elastic band or tied tightly with strong thin string. Alternatively, use two thicknesses of fine material, between which should be a knob of cotton-wool pressed flat so as to overlap the rim of the bottle, and tie tightly. The wine is left thus protected until all fermentation has ceased.

From the above the reader may imagine himself about to fight an army of microbes bent on frustrating his best efforts; he is quite right, but he can defeat that army at the expense of only a few minutes of his time.

Fermentation

Fermentation is indicated by a frothing (however slight) and a slight hissing noise or 'fizzing'. This is the complex action whereby the living organism of yeast breaks down the sugar into carbon dioxide and alcohol. The action of the yeast on the sugar continues until the volume of alcohol has reached somewhere between twelve and a half and fourteen per cent. At this stage the yeast organism is destroyed by the alcohol it has produced and fermentation ceases. This is what is known as a natural wine; most commercial products come under this category until they have been fortified. This period of fermenting in the tub is the danger time; therefore we must get fermentation over and done with as soon as possible – even at the risk of losing a little of the wine's bouquet.

We must then keep the brew warm. Our aim is to bring about ideal conditions in which the living organism and yeast cells can multiply more readily. Warmth ensures this. The more rapidly they multiply the more rapidly they convert the sugar into alcohol and, therefore, the sooner the yeast destroys itself.

Do not be tempted to keep a brew hot during fermentation: during warm weather any odd spot will do for a fermenting brew. During the winter, a warm spot in the kitchen or in an airing cupboard is as good as any.

After fourteen days' fermentation in a warm place, the wine is bottled or put into stone jars, and this is the time to add the isinglass.

Isinglass

Isinglass is not needed to clarify flower or fruit wines made with the recipes given in this book; these wines will clarify themselves quite readily within a few weeks of fermentation having ceased. Nor is isinglass an absolute need for clearing root wines, but I have found that root wines, and wines made from a mixture of roots and fruits, do clear more readily with the help of isinglass. For this reason you will see in certain recipes 'proceed with isinglass and bottling'.

When put into wine, isinglass forms an insoluble cloud which surrounds the minute solids in the wine and gradually forces them to the bottom of the bottle.

Apart from assisting the clearing process, isinglass helps to solidify the lees, thereby rendering them less easy to disturb while moving the bottles or when wine is poured from a bottle containing lees.

There are many methods of using isinglass, but the one I use myself with perfect results is as follows. Take one quart of the wine and warm it very slowly in a saucepan. Crumble one-eighth of an ounce of isinglass over the surface of this wine and then stir with a fork until all is dissolved, then pour it into the rest of the wine in a circling movement.

Many people advise dissolving the isinglass in a little water. As we have seen, ordinary tap-water quite often contains wild yeast; the very act, then, of using water might well ruin all our efforts to keep wild yeast out of the wine.

Bought from a chemist in half-ounce or one-ounce lots the amount required is easy to calculate, and this is usually plenty for one gallon of wine.

When the isinglass has been added, put the wine into *sterilized bottles or jars* and cover as already directed. The wine must then be returned to a warm place, and kept there until all fermentation has ceased.

If the wine were put in a cold place the yeast might go dormant and the wine cease to ferment; if it were later moved into a warm room, or the weather happened to turn very warm, the yeast would become active and start fermenting again. In a warm place fermentation cannot mislead us.

If by chance you notice that the top half-inch of wine has become crystal-clear, seal the bottles at once; for this is a clear indication that fermentation has ceased. Unfortunately we seldom get this invaluable guide.

When all fermentation has ceased – when no more tiny bubbles are rising to the surface – the yeast is dead. Fermentation cannot begin again unless wild yeast or bacteria get into the wine and begin that souring ferment I have mentioned. Perfect air-tight sealing at the earliest possible stage of production is essential.

Push the cork home hard and seal with sealing-wax. If screw-top bottles are available, use these by all means. I never use any other kind when I can get hold of them. Remember that the yeast is dead, so fermentation cannot begin again and explode the bottles or blow the corks unless wild yeast or bacteria reach the wine. Screw-top bottles are, then, the obvious choice.

The Clearing Process

As a general rule the clearing process will begin immediately fermentation has ceased. Clear divisions will be seen, each a slightly different shade. These will gradually fall to the bottom of the bottle as the wine eventually becomes clear.

If you use at least one clear-glass bottle, this process may be watched with interest. The top inch may become crystal-clear in a matter of days, yet it may be weeks before the top division finally reaches the bottom and becomes lees. The layer of sediment which will continue to build up in the bottles may remain an inch or so thick for some time, but this will eventually narrow down to barely half an inch. It may remain fluid, when it is very easily disturbed, or it may set so as to look like cheese.

At other times the clearing process will be seen as a gradual darkening, or in some cases brightening (depending on variety), of the colour of the wine; the layer of sediment will build up in the usual way, but without divisions.

When the wine is finally perfectly clear, we must prepare for the final bottling. No harm is done in leaving the wine on the lees until you wish to drink it, but this final bottling makes a tremendous difference to the wine's appearance and flavour. The clear wine should be siphoned off the lees into freshly sterilized bottles and sealed again at once with freshly sterilized corks or stoppers. The wine is then put away to mature and accumulate cobwebs. (For siphoning, see p. 18.)

If your wine seems somewhat slow to clear do not worry; put it somewhere where you cannot see it every day and get on with making the next brew. Many people will advise you to rebottle and keep rebottling until it is clear. Frequent racking – as it is called – merely invites contamination by bacteria. Wines will clear quite readily, provided they have been handled properly throughout and provided the jelly-bag straining was thorough.

Isinglass may be used as a last resort with a troublesome fruit wine, but I do not like this if it can be avoided for it takes down with it various chemical matter important to the flavour of the wine.

Cold – that is frosty weather – will usually clear obstinate wines.

I am at a loss to understand why some people are so impatient to get their wines clear. After all, wine is better for being a year old, and if it takes that long to clear I cannot see that anything has been lost. All wines improve with age; they become mellow, their flavour improves, their bouquet becomes more marked and their body more full. For all that, I expect you will drink your wine as soon as it has cleared. The period required for each brew to mature varies considerably: a safe rule is to allow six months for root wines and one year for wines made from fruit or flowers.

Storing

When the clear wine has been bottled and it is intended to keep it for more than three months, it must be borne in mind that corks dry out, and when this happens the shrinkage might cause cracking in the sealing-wax, with the result that tiny airholes will appear through which wild yeast and bacteria can attack the wine.

All bottles fitted with ordinary corks or cork-lined screw caps must be stored on their sides. This allows for the wine to keep the cork moist and so prevent shrinkage. Rubber-banded screw-stoppered bottles may be stored upright.

Having heard that wine should be stored at a certain temperature, which must remain constant throughout the year, many people go to much trouble and think up all sorts of ingenious devices to achieve that end. Authorities are divided in opinion as to the ideal temperature in which to store wines – probably because wines, like human beings, like what suits them best. Perhaps there is an ideal temperature for one kind of wine, but what suits the Eskimo does not suit the Australian aborigine, and never will.

In any case the aborigine and the Eskimo get changes in temperature and no harm comes to them – in fact, they seem to thrive on it. So why not let us regard our wines as being something like ourselves in that they are quite at home in such temperatures as we can give them?

Rapid changes are best avoided, of course (as with human beings); so if we can store our wines on a stone floor so much the better. If this is not possible, a cupboard on the north side of the house will do provided a chimney does not run through it.

But, darn it, a friend of mine stores three hundred bottles of some really magnificent wines in an attic which becomes unbearably hot in the summer and all but freezes out in the winter – and no harm ever comes to any of his wines.

Store your wines anywhere you can and don't worry.

When serving home-made wines, remember that they are best when served at room temperature, except for champagnes, which should be served cellar-cool or iced.

Siphoning and Bottling

It is almost impossible to pour clear wine from one bottle to another without stirring up the lees; it is a good plan, therefore, to siphon off the clear wine when rebottling.

Using about a yard and a half of surgical rubber tubing or plastic tubing, siphoning is a very simple operation. First put the bottles or jars of wine on a table and the empty bottles on a stool or box on the floor. Then put one end of the tubing in the first bottle of wine and suck the other end of the tube until the wine comes; pinch the tube at your lips and – holding on tight – put this end in the empty bottle and then let the wine flow. As the level of the wine falls, lower the tube into it, being careful not to let it touch the lees. When nearly all the wine has been transferred, pinch the tube at the neck of both bottles, put one end into the next bottle and allow the wine to flow again.

In this way a constant flow is maintained and you have bottles of crystal-clear wine. The sediment from each bottle may be put together; this will clear in time to leave a little more wine.

Now – What's Yours?

Most of you will already have heard of one or other home-made wine and will have decided which to make. For those who have not yet decided, preference for a 'port' or 'whisky' may be the deciding factor and this must rest with yourselves.

I would advise you only in this: make, say, a gallon or a half-gallon of a variety of wines and then decide which you prefer over a period of time. I have whittled my own preference down to nine different wines which I brew regularly according to season, leaving the dried fruit for the time when fresh fruit is not available and when roots – potatoes, etc. – are too fresh for wine-making purposes.

Note

Different recipes will call for a slightly different approach, but it must be remembered that whatever else has to be done, the brew must be kept in a warm place throughout the fermentation period, and that the process after fourteen days' fermentation in the tub is the same with all recipes.

Now select your recipe and go ahead with your wine-making, bearing in mind all that I have warned you about.

2

Root Wines

Many of the following root-wine recipes, and certain of the special recipes, call for the addition of wheat or raisins. When these are bought they are usually a little dirty and contain harmful bacteria. They should be washed in cold water, and then immersed – in a muslin or cloth bag – in boiling water for about a minute before using.

The first two recipes here, one for parsnip and another for potato wine, are recommended to the beginner. They clear very quickly, but they lack to some extent the fuller flavour and bouquet of the wines made under the recipes calling for rather more and interesting ingredients.

SIMPLE PARSNIP WINE

2½ lb. parsnips • ½ lb. raisins • ½ lb. sultanas
4 lb. sugar • 2 oranges • 2 lemons
1 oz. yeast • 5 quarts water

Scrub and grate the parsnips and put them in the water, bring just to boiling-point and simmer for five minutes. Strain and add the sugar at once and stir until all is dissolved. Then add the cut-up dried fruit and squeeze in the juice of the lemons and oranges. Allow to cool and then sprinkle the yeast on top and stir in. After fourteen days' fermentation, strain and proceed with isinglass and bottling.

Simple Potato Wine

 2 lb. potatoes • 1 lb. raisins • 4 oranges
 4 lb. sugar • 1 oz. yeast • 5 quarts water

Scrub and grate the potatoes and put them in the water. Bring slowly to boiling-point and strain at once. Add the sugar and stir until all is dissolved. Then put in the cut-up raisins and squeeze in the juice of the oranges. Allow to cool and then sprinkle the yeast on top and stir in. After fourteen days' fermentation, strain and proceed with isinglass and bottling.

Parsnip Wine

Very much like whisky when kept for a long time.

 4 lb. parsnips • 4 oranges • 4 lb. sugar
  1 oz. yeast • 5 quarts water

The preparation of the ingredients and the directions for making this wine are identical with those for making simple parsnip wine on page 20.

Mangold Wine (Mangel Wurzel)

A favourite among country folk. Mangolds are winter food for cattle, and may be obtained from farms. They make a really splendid wine which clears quite readily.

 5 lb. mangolds (one good-sized one)
 2 grapefruit • 4 lb. sugar • 1 oz. yeast
   5 quarts water

Do not peel the mangolds, but scrub them thoroughly and then cut them into small pieces or dice them, being careful not to lose any juice. Now cut up the grapefruit and place all the ingredients in the water (except the sugar and yeast). Bring slowly to the boil and simmer for twenty minutes, taking off all the scum that rises.

Strain into the fermenting vessel and add the sugar at once. Stir this until all is dissolved. Allow the wine to cool and then add the yeast. After fourteen days' fermentation proceed with isinglass and bottling.

Sugar-Beet Wine

For those who prefer a natural sweet wine.

    5 lb. sugar-beet • 3 oranges • 3 lemons
only 2 lb. sugar • 1 oz. yeast • 5 quarts water

Scrub and grate the unpeeled beet and put them into the water and bring slowly to the boil. Simmer gently for twenty minutes. Strain into the fermenting vessel and add the sugar at once. Then cut up the oranges and lemons into thin slices and float them on the surface of the brew. Allow the wine to cool and then add the yeast. After fourteen days' fermentation take off the sliced fruit and then proceed with isinglass and bottling.

Mixed-root Wines

Other delicious wines can be made from a mixture of roots. The quantity of each ingredient may be varied to suit individual tastes, but a reliable recipe is:

    2 lb. potatoes • 2 lb. parsnips • 4 oranges
    4 lb. sugar • 1 oz. yeast • 5 quarts water

The preparation of the ingredients and the directions for making this wine are the same as those for making simple potato wine on page 21.

Other delicious wines may be made from a varied mixture of roots, and by the same simple method. Suggested variations are offered here with the assurance that the resulting wines will be all you could wish for.

    2 lb. potatoes • 2 lb. carrots • 4 oranges
    4 lb. sugar • 1 oz. yeast • 5 quarts water

2 lb. carrots • 2 lb. beetroots • 2 oranges
2 lemons • 4 lb. sugar • 1 oz. yeast
5 quarts water

2 lb. carrots • 2 lb. parsnips • 4 oranges
4 lb. sugar • 1 oz. yeast • 5 quarts water

2 lb. potatoes • 2 lb. beetroots • 2 oranges
2 lemons • 4 lb. sugar • 1 oz. yeast
5 quarts water

These four variations are all worked to the directions given for simple potato wine on page 21.

BEETROOT WINE
Fine Old Tawny Port type

6 lb. beetroots (old shrivelled ones are best)
2 oranges • 2 lemons • 4 lb. sugar
1 oz. yeast • 5 quarts water

Scrub the beetroots clean and then slice them finely and put them in the water. Leave them to soak for one hour and then bring slowly to the boil and simmer gently for not more than ten minutes. Strain into the fermenting vessel and add the sugar at once. Stir well until all the sugar is dissolved. Cut the oranges and lemons into fine slices and let these float on the surface of the brew throughout the fourteen days' fermentation. Allow the brew to cool and then add the yeast. After fourteen days' fermentation take off the sliced fruit and then proceed with isinglass and bottling.

For Your Own Recipes

For Your Own Recipes

3
Wines From Other Vegetables

CELERY WINE

4 lb. celery • 3 lemons • 4 lb. sugar
1 oz. yeast • 5 quarts water

Wash the celery as you would for the table. The coarse outer sticks and the white leaves may be used provided all bruised or badly discoloured parts are first cut away. Cut the celery into small pieces and pour the boiling water over them. Then cut up the lemons and put them in with the rest. Leave to soak overnight. Bring gently to boiling-point and then cut off the heat. Strain into the fermenting vessel and add the sugar at once. Stir well, and when all the sugar is dissolved and the wine has cooled, add the yeast. After fourteen days' fermentation proceed with isinglass and bottling.

RUNNER-BEAN WINE

3 lb. runner beans (choose those you would use in the kitchen) • 2 grapefruit • 4 lb. sugar • 1 oz. yeast • 5 quarts water

Prepare the beans as you would for cooking and pour the boiling water over them. Into this mixture put the sliced grapefruit and allow the whole to soak overnight. Bring slowly just to boiling-point and strain into the fermenting vessel at once. Add the sugar immediately and stir until all is dissolved. Allow the wine to cool and then add the yeast. After fourteen days' fermentation proceed with isinglass and bottling.

Pea-shuck Wine

The shucks only are used and care should be taken to see that no peas enter the brew.

> 2½ lb. pea shucks • 1 grapefruit • 2 oranges
> 4 lb. sugar • 1 oz. yeast • 5 quarts water

Rinse the shucks under the tap and allow them to drain. Put them in the vessel used for boiling the ingredients and bruise them well. Cut up the grapefruit and oranges and place these with the pea shucks and then pour the boiling water over them. Allow to soak overnight. Bring just to boiling-point and then strain into the fermenting vessel and add the sugar at once. Stir until all the sugar is dissolved. When all is dissolved allow the wine to cool and add the yeast. After fourteen days' fermentation proceed with isinglass and bottling.

For Your Own Recipes

For Your Own Recipes

4
My Special Recipes

The recipes in this chapter are a little more expensive than most (though many of them contain wheat, which is quite cheap), but the wines that result from them are well worth the extra cost. They also offer wide scope for those who like to experiment (see Chapter 11, 'If You Experiment'). And finally there is much to be said for using ingredients that do not need a lot of scrubbing and boiling in their preparation.

Mr Noël Whitcomb's Carrot Whisky, and my own Jungle-Juice have won praise from all parts of the country. Their flavour, body and bouquet put them in the class of expensive spirits.

Carrot Whisky

The valuable contribution of Noël Whitcomb, the famous columnist of the Daily Mirror.

6 lb. carrots • 1 gallon water
1 tablespoonful raisins • 1 lb. wheat
1 oz. yeast • 2 oranges • 2 lemons • 4 lb. sugar

Scrub the carrots clean – don't peel them – and mash them. Put them in the water, bring to the boil, and simmer gently until very tender. Then strain off the liquid. (You can use the carrots for food – most dogs love them.) Into a bowl put the sugar and the sliced oranges and lemons and pour the hot liquid over them. Stir until the sugar is dissolved and stand until lukewarm. Then add the chopped raisins and wheat and sprinkle the yeast on top. Leave to ferment for fifteen days, then skim, strain and bottle.

To get the fullest flavour and strength, keep it for nearly a year – if you can.

Bravery's Extra Special Fine Old
JUNGLE-JUICE

4 lb. old potatoes • 6 oranges • ½ lb. raisins
1 lb. wheat • 4 lb. sugar • 1 oz. yeast
5 quarts water

Cut up the oranges and their peel and boil them gently for ten minutes in three pints of water. Then stand this aside. Do not peel the potatoes, but scrub them thoroughly. Then grate or slice them finely and bring to the boil in seven pints of water. *Simmer gently for not more than ten minutes, taking off any scum that rises.*

Strain into the fermenting tub and add the sugar at once. Stir until dissolved. Then add the wheat and cut-up raisins. Squeeze the oranges and then strain them, and add this liquid to the rest. While the liquid is still lukewarm sprinkle the yeast on top and stir in. After fourteen days' fermentation proceed with isinglass and bottling.

There is also an improved version of this recipe, which I call –

Bravery's Super Special Improved
JUNGLE-JUICE

Ingredients for *one and a half gallons.*

6 lb. old potatoes (the oldest procurable)
6 oranges • 1 lb. raisins • 1 lb. wheat
6 lb. sugar • 1 oz. yeast • 15 pints water
(1½ gals. plus 3 pints)

Cut up the oranges and their peel and boil them gently for ten minutes in the three extra pints of water. Then stand this aside. Do not peel the potatoes, but scrub them thoroughly. Then grate or slice finely and bring them to the boil in the rest of the water. *Simmer gently for not more than ten minutes, taking off any scum that rises.* Strain into the fermenting tub and add the sugar at once. Stir until dissolved. Then add the wheat and *whole* raisins. Squeeze the oranges, strain them, and add this liquid to the rest. Allow to cool and then sprinkle the yeast on top and stir in.

The raisins will float during fermentation and these should be taken up in handfuls each day and crushed. The wheat should be stirred up at the same time. After fourteen days' fermentation proceed with slightly more than one-eighth of an ounce of isinglass in a quart of warmed strained wine. Then go forward with bottling.

It will be noted that the number of oranges and the amount of wheat to be used is the same in both Jungle-Juice recipes.

Norah's Delight

2 lb. parsnips • 2 lb. carrots • $\frac{1}{2}$ lb. raisins
$\frac{1}{2}$ lb. wheat • 2 oranges • 2 lemons
4 lb. sugar • 1 oz. yeast • 5 quarts water

Scrub and grate the parsnips and carrots and bring them to the boil in one gallon of water. Simmer for ten minutes, taking off any scum that rises. Strain into the fermenting vessel and add the sugar at once. Stir until dissolved. Then cut up the oranges and lemons and boil them for ten minutes in the other quart of water. Strain and add this juice to the rest. Add the wheat and cut-up raisins and then set the brew aside to cool. When cool, sprinkle the yeast on top and stir in. After fourteen days' fermentation, strain and proceed with isinglass and bottling.

Westcott Schnapps

4 lb. parsnips • 3 oranges • 1 lb. raisins
1 lb. wheat • 1 oz. yeast • 3½ lb. sugar
5 quarts water

Scrub the parsnips clean and then slice them finely and bring them to the boil in one gallon of water. Simmer gently for not more than ten minutes, taking off any scum that rises. Strain into the fermenting vessel and add the sugar at once. Stir until all is dissolved. Cut up the oranges and boil them for ten minutes in the extra quart of water. Strain, and add this juice to the rest. Add the wheat and whole raisins and then allow the liquid to cool and add the yeast.

The raisins will float during fermentation and these should be taken in handfuls and crushed three times during the first seven days of fermentation. The wheat should be stirred at the same time. After fourteen days' fermentation, proceed with isinglass and bottling.

Canadian Whisky

2 lb. wheat • 2 lb. raisins • 4 oranges
4 lb sugar • 1 oz. yeast • 5 quarts water

Bring the water to boiling-point and cut off the heat at once. Pour in the sugar and stir until dissolved. Then add the wheat and cut-up raisins. Cut up the oranges and squeeze their juice into the rest. Work the peel well between the fingers to press out the oil in it – much flavour is obtained from this. Allow to cool and then sprinkle the yeast on top and stir in. After fourteen days' fermentation, strain and proceed with isinglass and bottling.

Dorking Whisky

12 medium-sized oranges • 1 lb. wheat
4 lb. sugar • 1 oz. yeast • 5 quarts water

Cut up the oranges into small pieces, pour the boiling water over them, and leave to soak for four days. Crush well with the hands each day. Then bring to boiling-point, strain into the fermenting vessel and add the sugar at once. Stir until all the sugar is dissolved and add the wheat. When the liquid has cooled, sprinkle the yeast on top and stir in. After fourteen days' fermentation, strain and proceed with isinglass and bottling.

Wheat Wine

3 lb. wheat • 2 oranges • 2 lemons
4 lb. sugar • 1 oz. yeast • 5 quarts water

Pour the sugar into the boiling water and cut off the heat at once. Stir until the sugar is dissolved and pour in the wheat. Cut up the oranges and lemons and squeeze them into the brew. Cut up the rinds and let these float on the brew during fermentation. Allow the brew to cool and then add the yeast. After fourteen days' fermentation, take off the fruit rinds and then proceed with isinglass and bottling.

Orange and Raisin Wine

12 medium-sized oranges • 1 lb. raisins
4 lb. sugar • 1 oz. yeast • 5 quarts water

Cut up the oranges and bring them to the boil in the five quarts of water. Simmer gently for ten minutes. Strain into the fermenting vessel and add the sugar at once. Stir until all is dissolved and put in the raisins. Allow the wine to cool, sprinkle the yeast on top and stir in.

The raisins will float during fermentation and these should be crushed by hand two or three times during the first seven days of fermentation; after which the brew is left undisturbed for the remainder of the fourteen days' fermentation period. After fourteen days' fermentation, strain and proceed with isinglass and bottling.

Scotch Bravery

1½ lb. wheat • 2 lb. raisins • 3 oranges
3½ lb. sugar • 1 oz. yeast • 9 pints water
1 tablespoonful freshly made strong tea

Pour the sugar into the boiling water and cut off the heat. Stir until all is dissolved and then pour into the fermenting vessel. Wash the wheat and raisins in cold water and then pour them into some boiling water. Bring to the boil again, strain, throw away the water and put the wheat and raisins into the sugar water which is already in the fermenting vessel.

Halve the oranges and squeeze their juice into the prepared mixture. Allow the brew to cool and then sprinkle the yeast on top and stir in.

During fermentation crush the raisins by hand and stir up the wheat every other day for fourteen days. This operation must be carried out quickly, and the brew covered and tied down again at once. After fourteen days' fermentation, strain the wine, add a tablespoonful of freshly made strong tea to the strained wine and bottle it.

Directions thereafter are the same as those already given in this book.

'Don't Mind if I Do' Port

4 lb. sugar • 1 oz. yeast • 1 gallon water
and *one* of the following:
4 lb. elderberries • 6 lb. damsons
8 lb. red plums • 4½ lb. blackberries

Crush the fruits, pour the cold water over them, and crush well with the hands as often and as much as you like during the following forty-eight hours. Then strain through fine muslin and put the juice through a jellybag or flannel.

Bring the juice to boiling-point and simmer for three

minutes, taking off all the scum that rises. Pour the hot juice over the sugar and stir until all the sugar is dissolved. Allow the brew to cool, sprinkle the yeast on top and stir in. After fourteen days' fermentation proceed as for 'Scotch Bravery' (page 31).

Peach Brandy

4 lb. peaches (ripe to the point of tenderness)
½ lb. dates · 1 lb. kibbled maize · ½ lb. wheat
grated rind of 1 orange · 4 lb. sugar
9 pints water · 1 oz. yeast

Halve the peaches and crush them well. Pour the boiling water over them and leave to soak for forty-eight hours, crushing well several times. Strain through fine muslin and squeeze the pulp well. Put the juice through a jelly-bag and boil it for two minutes. Pour the hot juice over the sugar and stir until all is dissolved, then add the broken-up dates and cereals. Grate the orange peel over the brew. Allow to cool, then sprinkle the yeast on top and stir in. Cover, and ferment for fourteen days, after which strain and proceed with bottling.

Orange Brandy

12 large oranges (or their equivalent)
½ lb. dates · ½ lb. raisins · 1 lb. kibbled maize
4 lb. sugar · 1 gallon water · 1 oz. yeast

Halve the oranges and squeeze out as much juice as possible. Fold and refold the peel between the fingers to squeeze out the oil. Do all this over the water so that nothing is lost. Then put the spent orange halves in the water and soak for twenty-four hours. Strain, and put the juice through a jelly-bag. Bring the strained juice to boiling-point and simmer gently for two minutes. Pour the hot juice over the sugar and stir until all is dissolved. Then add the raisins, kibbled maize and dates and stir well in.

Mead

Allow the brew to cool, then sprinkle the yeast on top and stir in. Cover as directed and ferment for fourteen days, after which proceed with bottling.

Mead

Mead is one of the oldest of drinks, and is brewed today, in many different forms, in Cornwall. To make the best sort, a specially prepared mead yeast is recommended. For simple mead – one resembling wine – baker's yeast may be used.

4 lb. English honey • ½ oz. root ginger
pared rinds of 2 lemons • 1 oz. yeast
1 gallon water • 1 oz. hops

Put the honey, ginger, hops and pared lemon rinds into the water and boil for forty-five minutes, making up with boiled water what you lose by evaporation. Allow the mead to cool, then add the yeast and pour into a stone or glass jar. This should be covered as directed for wines and fermentation allowed to carry itself to its end; then cork and seal.

Isinglass may be needed if the mead has not cleared at the end of six months; if so, add a little dissolved in boiled water.

Fruit-Flavoured Mead (dry)

Strictly speaking this is not mead, but many people like it and I recommend it to those who like a 'dryish' fruit-flavoured wine with a unique flavour underlying that of the fruit.

Redcurrants, blackcurrants, elderberries and loganberries are the best fruits to use, but if these are unobtainable try stone fruits such as plums, and use half again the amount given for the soft fruit.

2 lb. English honey • 3 lb. soft fruit of your choice
½ lb. raisins (or 1 lb. if you can spare them)
9 pints water • 1 oz. yeast

If you do not like too dry a wine you should add 1½ lb. of sugar as directed.

Crush the fruit, pour half the cold water over them, and leave to soak overnight. Strain through fine muslin and put the juice through a jelly-bag. Bring this juice to boiling-point and simmer for three minutes.

If using the sugar, pour the hot juice over this and stir until all is dissolved. If not using sugar, leave the juice to cool. Boil the honey for forty-five minutes in half of the water, and if too much has been boiled away make up with boiled water to the correct amount. Add the raisins and the strained fruit juice and leave to cool. When cool, add the yeast.

Cover as directed and ferment for fourteen days in the tub; then strain, crushing the raisins well, and proceed with bottling.

Dissolve a little isinglass in boiled water (or part of the wine) and add this if the 'mead' has not become clear within six months.

Parsley Brandy

Parsley will grow almost anywhere, especially along edges of gravel paths, or even in window boxes provided it gets a few hours' sunshine now and again. A packet of seed will produce more than is needed to make ten gallons of brew throughout the season, so anyone who wishes to make parsley brandy can easily do so.

¾ lb. parsley • 3½ lb. sugar • 2 lemons
3 oranges • ½ oz. bruised ginger (optional)
¼ lb. raisins • ½ lb. wheat • 1 gallon water
1 oz. yeast

Chop the parsley, being careful not to lose any juice, and pour the boiling water over this. Leave to soak for twelve hours and then strain through three thicknesses of fine muslin or put through a jelly-bag. Bring the strained liquid to the boil and simmer for five minutes. Pour the hot liquid over the sugar and stir until all is dissolved, then add the wheat and raisins. Cut up the oranges and lemons and squeeze their juice into the liquid. When cool, add the yeast. Cover as directed and ferment for fourteen days, leaving the spent halves on the surface of the brew for seven days. Strain, and proceed with bottling.

Note: if ginger is used this should be boiled with the parsley water.

Apricot Brandy

If fresh apricots are not available use dried apricots in the proportions advised.

> 4 lb. fresh apricots or 5–6 lb. dried apricots
> 1 gallon water (add an extra pint if dried apricots are used)
> ½ lb. sultanas • 1 lb. wheat or kibbled maize (or ½ lb. each)
> 4 lb. sugar • 1 oz. yeast

If dried apricots are used, soak them overnight, crush them well, and then leave to soak for another twelve hours before proceeding as for fresh apricots. If using fresh apricots, halve the fruits and save half the stones. Crush the fruits well and pour the water over them, leaving to soak for twenty-four hours, crushing well several times. Give a final thorough crushing before straining through fine muslin. Put the juice through a jelly-bag, bring slowly to the boil and simmer for four minutes. Pour the hot juice over the sugar and stir until all is dissolved. Then add the sultanas, raisins and cereals. Allow to cool, then sprinkle the yeast on top and stir in. Put in the apricot stones (if fresh apricots were used). Cover as directed and ferment for fourteen days, occasionally stirring up the cereals and crushing the sultanas. Then proceed with bottling.

Barley Water

This is non-alcoholic.

2 oz. pearl barley • 5 pints water

Wash the barley in cold water and boil it in a quart of different water for five minutes. Strain, and throw the water away. Then put the barley in five pints of water and boil gently until only half the original amount remains. Strain, and allow to cool.

This should produce two pints of barley water.

Lemon Barley Water

Proceed as for barley water and add the juice of one lemon to each pint of barley water at the time of final straining.

Orange Barley Water

Proceed as for *lemon barley water* (above), using oranges instead of lemons.

Plum Brandy

Note: For Plum Wine see pages 52–3. But a plum wine – or, for that matter, any other fruit wine – with wheat added becomes what home wine-makers call a brandy, although there is no distilled spirit added. So plum wine with wheat added becomes plum 'brandy'.

A real brandy is, of course, a spirit resulting from distillation. I very often advise against using cereals in fruit wine recipes for the simple reason that people making wine want wine and not a wine bearing a resemblance to one that has had spirit added. Cereals have the effect of adding that spirituousness that one associates with fortified wines.

5–8 lb. red plums (according to taste)
1 lb. wheat • ½ lb. kibbled maize
3½–4½ lb. sugar (according to the amount of plums used)
1 gallon water • 1 oz. yeast

Halve and stone the plums. Crush them and pour the cold water over them. Leave to soak for twenty-four hours, crushing with the hands several times during that time. Strain through fine muslin and put the juice through a jelly-bag. Bring the juice to boiling-point and simmer for five minutes, taking off any scrum that rises. Strain the hot juice over the sugar and stir until all is dissolved. Add the wheat and kibbled maize (which, as we have seen, must be washed and then boiled for a few minutes). Allow the brew to cool, then sprinkle the yeast on top and stir in. Cover as directed and ferment for fourteen days, after which, strain the wine and proceed with bottling.

Note: some people prefer this wine when it has been fermented with half the stones taken from the plums.

Rhubarb Brandy

6 lb. rhubarb • 1 lb. dates • 1 lb. barley
1 gallon water • 4 lb. sugar • 1 oz. yeast

Wipe the rhubarb clean with a damp cloth, cut into small pieces, and then crush with a rolling-pin. Place the rhubarb in the water and allow to soak for twenty-four hours, crushing as much as possible during that time. Strain through muslin and put the juice through a jelly-bag. Bring the juice to boiling-point and simmer for three minutes. Strain on to the sugar and stir until all the sugar is dissolved, then add the cut-up dates and the barley. Allow the brew to cool, sprinkle the yeast on top and stir in. Cover as directed and ferment for fourteen days, after which strain and proceed with the first bottling.

Rhubarb Brandy (another version)

6 lb. rhubarb · 3 oranges · 1 lb. kibbled maize
4 lb. sugar · 1 gallon water · 1 oz. yeast

Wipe the rhubarb clean with a damp cloth, cut into small pieces, and crush with a rolling-pin. Put the rhubarb in the water and allow to soak for twenty-four hours, crushing as much as possible during that time. Strain through fine muslin and put the juice through a jelly-bag. Bring the juice to boiling-point and simmer for three minutes. Strain on to the sugar and stir until all is dissolved.

Then add the kibbled maize and the juice of the oranges. Allow the brew to cool, sprinkle the yeast on top and stir in. Cut the spent orange halves into small pieces and float these on the brew during the whole of the fermentation period in the tub. Cover as directed and ferment for fourteen days, after which strain and proceed with bottling.

Mulberry Brandy

4 lb. mulberries · 1 lb. wheat · 4 lb. sugar
1 gallon water · 1 oz. yeast

Crush the mulberries and pour the water over them. Allow to soak overnight and then crush well by hand and strain through fine muslin. Put the juice through a jelly-bag and bring this strained juice to boiling-point. Simmer for three or four minutes – not longer – taking off all the scum that rises. Pour the hot juice over the sugar and stir until all dissolved. Add the wheat. Allow the brew to cool and then sprinkle the yeast on top and stir in. Cover as directed and ferment for fourteen days (stirring up the wheat once or twice during this period). Strain and proceed with bottling.

Elderberry Brandy

4 lb. elderberries • ½ lb. raisins • 1 lb. wheat
4 lb. sugar • 1 gallon water • 1 oz. yeast

Strip the elderberries from the stalks and crush them. Pour the cold water over them and allow to stand for twenty-four hours, stirring and crushing by hand several times during that period. Crush well before straining through fine muslin. Put the strained juice through a jelly-bag. Bring just to boiling-point and simmer for three or four minutes, taking off all the scum that rises. Pour the hot juice over the sugar and stir until all is dissolved. Add the wheat and raisins. Allow the brew to cool. Then sprinkle the yeast on top and stir in. Cover as directed and ferment for fourteen days. Strain and proceed with bottling.

Raspberry Brandy

5 lb. raspberries (or 3–4 lb., making up with raisins and dates in equal proportions)
1 large grapefruit (or 2 oranges and 2 lemons)
4 lb. sugar (to full quantity of raspberries)
or
3½ lb. sugar (if raisins and dates used as make-weight)
1 gallon water • 1 lb. wheat • 1 oz. yeast

Crush the raspberries and pour the water over them. Leave to soak for forty-eight hours, stirring and crushing by hand occasionally. Strain through fine muslin and put the juice through a jelly-bag. Bring the strained juice to boiling-point and simmer for three minutes, taking off all the scum that rises. Pour the hot juice over the sugar and stir until all is dissolved. Then add the wheat (and the raisins and dates if you are using them). Halve the grapefruit (or the oranges and lemons), and squeeze the juice into the brew. Allow it to cool and then sprinkle the yeast on top and stir in.

Cut the spent halves into small pieces and float these on the surface of the brew while it ferments for fourteen days; stir up the wheat (and crush the dates and raisins if you are using them), occasionally during the fermentation. After fourteen days, strain and then proceed with bottling.

This wine sometimes takes a little longer than usual to clear, but it is well worth waiting another month for.

Loganberry Brandy

4 lb. loganberries · 1 lb. wheat or kibbled maize
(or ½ lb. each)
1 lemon (or 1 orange) · 4 lb. sugar
1 gallon water · 1 oz. yeast

Crush the fruit well by hand or press through a colander or sieve. Pour the cold water over the crushed fruit and allow to soak for forty-eight hours, stirring occasionally. Strain through fine muslin and put the juice through a jelly-bag. Bring the juice to boiling-point and simmer very gently for four minutes, taking off all the scum that rises. Pour the hot juice over the sugar and stir until all is dissolved. Then add the wheat or maize and the juice of the lemon or orange, discarding the spent halves. Allow the brew to cool and then sprinkle the yeast on top and stir in. Cover as directed and ferment for fourteen days, stirring up the wheat occasionally. After fourteen days' fermentation, strain and proceed with bottling.

Cherry Brandy

If handled properly this recipe should provide a good imitation of the very popular – and very expensive – commercial product, especially if a quarter-bottle of brandy can be spared at the final bottling stage.

6 lb. Morello cherries • 1 lb. red currants
1 lb. wheat • 4 lb. sugar • 1 gallon water
1 oz. yeast

Remove the stalks, rinse the fruit under a fast-running tap and then crush well. Pour the cold water over the crushed fruit and allow to soak for forty-eight hours. Crush well before straining through fine muslin. Squeeze the pulp to get the maximum juice and then put this through a jelly-bag. Bring to boiling-point and simmer for seven minutes, taking off all the scum that rises. Strain the hot juice over the sugar and stir until all is dissolved.

Now treat the red currants in exactly the same way, keeping the juice separate and using no water. When the red-currant juice is cool, pour in the wheat. Then sprinkle the yeast on top of the juice-and-wheat mixture.

Cover both brews as directed. When fermentation has been going on for about forty-eight hours pour the fermenting brew into the cherry-water, and allow fermentation to continue the full fourteen days' period. Then strain and proceed with bottling.

This is greatly improved by the addition of a quarter-bottle or half-bottle of brandy added to the bulk after it has been siphoned off the lees. If brandy is added, the wine should be kept for a total of nine months at least. The addition of brandy is not essential.

GINGER WINE

Non-alcoholic. Ingredients are obtainable from any chemist.

2–4 drams essence of ginger (according to strength of flavour desired)
1 dessertspoonful lemon essence
½ oz. capsicum • 1–1½ oz. burnt sugar
½ oz. tartaric acid • 3½ lb. sugar • 7 pints water

Boil the water and dissolve the sugar in it. When the sugar is dissolved, add all the ingredients except the tartaric acid. Stir all well together and allow to stand for twelve hours. Then take a little of the 'wine' and in this dissolve the tartaric acid. Mix well into the rest, and bottle for one week before using.

This will not keep indefinitely.

Note: your chemist may require you to provide a bottle for the ingredients, except for the tartaric acid which will be packed separately.

Ginger Wine

1 oz. whole ginger (mild flavour)
or
1½ oz. whole ginger (fairly-strong flavour)
or
2 oz. whole ginger (strong flavour)
3½ lb. sugar • 2 oranges • 2 lemons
½ lb. sultanas • ½ lb. raisins • 1 gallon water
1 oz. yeast

Slice the lemons and oranges finely, bruise the ginger and put all together in the water. Bring slowly to the boil and simmer gently for fifteen minutes – no longer. Strain the liquid over the sugar (a jelly-bag is not needed here – three thicknesses of muslin will do), and stir until all the sugar is dissolved. Then add the dried fruit. Allow the brew to cool, then sprinkle the yeast on top and stir in. Cover as directed and ferment for fourteen days, after which proceed with straining and bottling. As the ginger has to be boiled, this wine may take rather longer than usual to clear, but a slight cloudiness will not be so noticeable because of the colour.

If you insist upon a crystal-clear wine, try using ginger essence as in the ginger wine (non-alcoholic) recipe above.

MY SPECIAL RECIPES

The following two recipes came to me from Mr. Toleman, of Gloucester. He wrote that he had only just begun to make wines but already had fifty bottles in store. Obviously an addict to home wine-making; I wish him every success.

Rice Wine

3 lb. rice • 1 lb. raisins • 3 lb. sugar
1 oz. yeast • 5 quarts water

Bring the water to boiling-point and cut off the heat at once. Pour in the sugar and stir until dissolved. Then add the rice and chopped raisins. Allow the mixture to cool and sprinkle the yeast on top and stir in. After fourteen days' fermentation strain and proceed with isinglass and bottling.

Wheat Wine

1 lb. wheat • 2 lb. sultanas • 1 lb. old potatoes
2 grapefruit • 4 lb. sugar • 1 oz. yeast
5 quarts water

Scrub, grate and boil the potatoes in four pints of water for ten minutes, taking off any scum that rises. Strain the potatoes and set the water aside. Boil the rest of the water and pour in the sugar. Stir until dissolved and then put the two liquids together. Add the chopped sultanas. Allow the brew to cool and then sprinkle the yeast on top and stir in. Slice the grapefruit finely, being careful not to lose any juice, and float them on the brew during the whole of the fermentation period. After fourteen days' fermentation strain and proceed with isinglass and bottling.

5
Fruit Wines

It will be noted that in the following fruit wine recipes the soaking period is very short. If readers fear that they won't get much goodness from the fruit in that little time, let me assure them that they will get all they need. Long periods of soaking merely invite the wild yeast on the fruit and in the air to begin that 'undesirable ferment' I have already mentioned. The short soaking period is a safeguard against this, and the boiling of the juices destroys the yeast organisms but at the same time is not long enough to give the wine a 'cooked-fruit' flavour. (For wines with this flavour, see p. 129.)

The soaking fruit mixtures must be covered well and kept in a cool place until the time comes for straining.

ELDERBERRY WINE

Rich port-style – full bodied.

There are numerous recipes for making this wine. The one I myself use most frequently is the first, but I often make elderberry-and-prune wine and elderberry-and-grape wine.

Do not gather the berries from railway embankments where steam trains are in service, since traces of the smoke give an unpleasant taste to the wine. If the berries are gathered from the side of a busy road, they may need to be rinsed. Gather them when the clusters are fully ripe.

3 lb. elderberries (weighed without stalks)
4 lb. sugar • 1 oz. yeast • 1 gallon water

Crush the berries, pour one gallon of cold water over them, and leave to soak overnight. Strain through fine muslin and put the strained juice through a jelly-bag. If slow to drain, leave overnight. Then bring the strained juice slowly to boiling-point and simmer for five minutes, taking off any scum that rises. Put the sugar into the fermenting vessel and pour the hot liquid over it. Stir until all the sugar is dissolved. Allow the brew to cool and then sprinkle the yeast on top and stir in. Cover as directed and leave to ferment for fourteen days before bottling.

Elderberry Wine

3 quarts elderberries (measured without stalks)
4 lb. sugar • 1 oz. yeast • 1 gallon water

Boil half the water and when it has cooled pour it over the crushed berries. Leave to soak overnight. Strain through fine muslin and put the strained juice through a jelly-bag. Mix the pulp with the other half-gallon of water, strain again and put this strained juice through the jelly-bag, then put the juices together. Bring slowly to boiling-point, taking off any scum that rises, and simmer for two minutes. Pour into the fermenting vessel and add the sugar at once. Stir until all the sugar is dissolved. Allow the brew to cool and then sprinkle the yeast on top and stir in.

Cover as directed and leave to ferment for fourteen days before bottling.

Elderberry Wine

2½ lb. elderberries (weighed without stalks)
1 gallon water • 3 lb. sugar • 1 oz. yeast

Crush the berries and pour the boiling water over them (the little pectin that *might* get into the liquid will not matter). Stir well and leave to soak for twelve hours.

Crush well and then strain through fine muslin and put the juice through a jelly-bag. Bring this just to boiling-point and cut off the heat at once. Pour into the fermenting vessel and add the sugar immediately, stirring until all is dissolved. Allow the brew to cool and then sprinkle the yeast on top and stir in. Cover as directed and leave to ferment for fourteen days; after which proceed with bottling.

Elderberry and Damson Wine

It is not always that these fruits ripen at just the right time, but when they do, the following recipe may be relied upon to produce a very good imitation of port.

> 2 lb. elderberries (weighed without stalks)
> 2 lb. damsons · 4 lb. sugar · 1 oz. yeast
> 1 gallon water

Crush both fruits and put them together. Boil the water and let it cool a bit, then pour it over the fruit pulp. Leave to soak overnight, then strain through fine muslin, put the juice through a jelly-bag and allow to drain. Bring this strained juice just to boiling-point and simmer for five minutes. Pour into the fermenting vessel and add the sugar at once. Stir until all the sugar is dissolved. Allow the brew to cool and then sprinkle the yeast on top and stir in. Cover as directed, leave to ferment for fourteen days, and then proceed with bottling.

Elderberry and Prune Wine

> 1½ lb. elderberries · 2 lb. dried prunes
> 3½ lb. sugar · 9 pints water · 1 oz. yeast

Pour half a gallon of boiling water over the prunes and leave them to soak overnight. At the same time crush the elderberries and, in a separate vessel, pour another half-gallon of water over them and leave to soak overnight. Crush both mixtures well and put them together, then strain through fine muslin and put the juice through a jelly-bag. Put the extra pint of water into the fruit pulp, strain, and put this also through the jelly-bag. Bring the strained juice just to boiling-point and simmer for two minutes. Pour into the fermenting vessel and add the sugar at once. Stir until all the sugar is dissolved. Allow the brew to cool and then sprinkle the yeast on top and stir in. Cover as directed and leave to ferment for fourteen days before bottling.

Elderberry and Raisin Wine

2 lb. elderberries (weighed without stalks)
1 lb. raisins • 3½ lb. sugar • 1 oz. yeast
9 pints water

Crush the elderberries and pour over them one gallon of water that has been boiled and cooled; leave this to soak overnight. Strain through fine muslin and put the juice through a jelly-bag. Pour the extra pint of water over the fruit pulp and put this through the jelly-bag. Bring the strained juice just to boiling-point and simmer for two minutes, taking off any scum that rises. Pour into the fermenting vessel and add the sugar at once. Stir until all the sugar is dissolved and then put in the chopped raisins. Allow the brew to cool and then sprinkle the yeast on top and stir in. Cover as directed and leave to ferment for fourteen days, then strain and proceed with bottling.

Blackcurrant and Rhubarb Appetizer

3 lb. rhubarb • 1 lb. blackcurrants • 4 lb. sugar
1 oz. yeast • 1 gallon water

Wipe the rhubarb clean with a damp cloth and then crush the sticks with a rolling-pin. Begin in the middle of each stick and work in a rocking – forward and backward – movement, being careful not to lose any juice. Put the juice and fruit pulp into the water with the crushed blackcurrants and leave to soak overnight. Crush well, strain through fine muslin, and put the juice through a jelly-bag. Bring the strained juice just to boiling-point and simmer for three minutes. Pour into the fermenting vessel and add the sugar at once. Stir until all the sugar is dissolved. Allow the brew to cool and then sprinkle the yeast on top and stir in. Leave to ferment for fourteen days and bottle.

Crab-Apple Wine

1 gallon crab-apples • 4 lb. sugar • 1 oz. yeast
1 gallon water

Chop the crab-apples without coring or peeling them and pour the cold water over them. Leave to soak for twelve hours, stirring every so often.

Crush well with the hands and then strain through fine muslin and put the juice through a jelly-bag. Bring the juice to boiling-point and simmer for five minutes. Pour into the fermenting vessel and add the sugar at once. Stir until all the sugar is dissolved. Allow the brew to cool and then sprinkle the yeast on top and stir in.

Cover as directed and leave to ferment for fourteen days. Bottle.

Crab-Apple Wine

3 quarts crab-apples • 1 lb. raisins
9 pints water • $3\frac{1}{2}$ lb. sugar • 1 oz. yeast

Chop the crab-apples without coring or peeling them, and soak them in the water overnight, stirring occasionally. Work the pieces of fruit between the fingers to crush as much as possible and then strain through fine muslin and put the juice through a jelly-bag. Bring the juice just to boiling-point and simmer for five minutes. Pour into the fermenting vessel and add the sugar at once. Stir until all the sugar is dissolved. Then cut up or chop the raisins and add them to the brew. Allow the brew to cool and then sprinkle the yeast on top and stir in. Cover as directed and leave to ferment for fourteen days, then proceed with bottling.

Strawberry Wine

3 lb. strawberries • 2 grapefruit • 2½ lb. sugar
1 oz. yeast • 1 gallon water

Boil the water, and while it is still warm, pour it over the crushed strawberries. Leave to soak for a few hours, stirring occasionally. Crush well and put the pulp through a jelly-bag. Halve the grapefruit and squeeze the juice into the strained strawberry juice. Then bring this to the boil and simmer for two minutes. Pour into the fermenting vessel and add the sugar at once. Stir until the sugar is dissolved. Allow the brew to cool and then sprinkle the yeast on top and stir in. Cover as directed and ferment for fourteen days; after which proceed with bottling.

Blackcurrant Wine

3 lb. blackcurrants • 3 lb. sugar • 1 oz. yeast
1 gallon water

Crush the blackcurrants, pour the boiling water over them, and then leave to soak for forty-eight hours. Crush well, put the pulp through a jelly-bag and allow to drain. Bring the juice just to boiling-point and cut off the heat at once. Add the sugar and stir until all is dissolved. Allow to cool and then sprinkle the yeast on top and stir in. Cover as directed and leave to ferment for fourteen days; after which proceed with bottling.

Grape Wine

Either black, green or amber grapes may be used for this recipe and the resulting wine will suit almost every taste.

4 lb. grapes • 3½ lb. sugar • 1 oz. yeast
1 gallon water

Strip the grapes from the stalks and then crush them by hand. Pour the boiling water over them and leave to soak for forty-eight hours. Strain and put the juice through a jelly-bag. Allow to drain and then pour into the fermenting vessel and add the sugar. Stir until the sugar is dissolved – this will take quite some time with cold grape-juice. When all the sugar is dissolved sprinkle the yeast on top and stir in. Cover, and ferment for fourteen days; after which proceed with bottling.

Grape Wine

(using black grapes)

3 lb. good-quality grapes • 3 lb. sugar
1 oz. yeast • 1 gallon water

Crush the grapes by hand and set them aside in the fermenting vessel. Bring the water to boiling-point and pour in the sugar. When the water reaches boiling-point again and when the sugar is all dissolved, cut off the heat and pour the sugar liquid over the grapes. Allow the mixture to cool and then sprinkle the yeast on top and stir it in. Cover as directed and ferment for fourteen days, strain it and proceed with bottling.

An Old Recipe

An old recipe for grape wine belonging to my late grandmother begins:

'Procure four stones of the finest quality grapes and one gallon of the tendrils of the vine chopped fine. Produce enough leaves of the vine to make a bed for the grapes. Make the bed in the sun and lay the grapes upon it. When the leaves begin to curl put the grapes and tendrils in a vessel and hang it over a log fire. Bring the grapes to the temperature of blood . . . The best grapes are those from a vine fed on pigs' blood. . . . Into a prepared tun put eight gallons of the softest spring-water . . .'

I bet that was good stuff.

Grape and Elderberry Wine

2 lb. elderberries • 2 lb. black grapes
3½ lb. sugar • 1 oz. yeast • 1 gallon water

Crush the fruits and set them aside in one vessel. Bring the water to boiling-point and in it dissolve the sugar. Stir until the sugar is dissolved and pour this hot liquid over the fruit mixture. Allow to cool and then sprinkle the yeast on top and stir in. Cover as directed and ferment for fourteen days; strain, and proceed with bottling.

Grape and Elderberry Wine

3 lb. elderberries • 1 lb. green or amber grapes
3½ lb. sugar • 1 oz. yeast • 1 gallon water

Crush the grapes and elderberries and pour half the boiling water over them, leaving to soak overnight. Strain the pulp through a jelly-bag and set the juice aside. Mix the pulp with the other half-gallon of water, stir well and put this through the jelly-bag. Mix the two strained juices together and add the sugar, stirring until all the sugar is dissolved, and then sprinkle the yeast on top and stir in. Cover, and ferment for fourteen days; then proceed with bottling.

Damson Wine

5 lb. damsons (weighed with the stones)
3½ lb. sugar • 1 oz. yeast • 1 gallon water

Boil the water and allow it to cool a little. Crush the damsons and pour the water over them. Leave to soak for forty-eight hours, stirring occasionally. Then crush well, strain, and put the strained juice through a jelly-bag. Bring the strained juice just to boiling-point and simmer for five minutes. Put the sugar into the fermenting vessel and pour the hot liquid over it. Stir until all the sugar is dissolved. Allow to cool and then sprinkle the yeast on top and stir in. Cover as directed and ferment for fourteen days; after which, proceed with bottling.

WHORTLEBERRY WINE

A Hertfordshire recipe. Whortleberries grow wild in many parts of the country, and for the price of four pounds of sugar a gallon of 'port' may be made.

3½ lb. whortleberries · 3½ lb. sugar
1 oz. yeast · 1 gallon water

Boil half the water, let it cool a little, and then pour it over the crushed berries. Leave to soak for forty-eight hours. Put the fruit pulp through a jelly-bag and set the juice aside. Pour the other half-gallon of water into the fruit pulp and let it drain. Add the two juices together and bring just to boiling-point. Put the sugar into the fermenting vessel and pour the hot liquid over it. Stir until all the sugar is dissolved. Allow to cool and then sprinkle the yeast on top and stir in. Cover as directed and ferment for fourteen days; after which proceed with bottling.

VICTORIA OR OTHER PLUM WINE

This recipe and its working directions are also suitable for all other varieties of plum wines. Merely substitute for Victoria plums those available to you.

6 lb. plums (weighed with the stones)
3½ lb. sugar . 1 oz. yeast · 1 gallon water

Halve the plums, remove the stones and crush the fruit with the hands. Boil half the water and pour this, when cool, over the fruit pulp. Leave to soak for four or five hours. Strain and then mix the other half of the water with the pulp, and then strain the two juices through a jelly-bag. This should produce about one gallon of good clear juice. Bring the juice just to boiling-point and while still hot pour it over the sugar in the fermenting vessel. Stir until all the sugar is dissolved. Allow the brew to cool and then sprinkle the yeast on top and stir in. Cover as directed and ferment for fourteen days; after which, proceed with bottling.

Greengage Wine

4½ lb. greengages • 3 lb. sugar • 1 gallon water
1 oz. yeast

Cut the gages down one side, stone them and put them in the water. Leave to soak for twelve hours and then crush, strain and put the pulp through a jelly-bag. Bring the juice just to boiling-point and simmer for five minutes. Then pour the hot juice over the sugar and stir until all the sugar is dissolved. Cover as directed and ferment for fourteen days; after which proceed with bottling.

Red Currant Wine

4 lb. red currants • 3½ lb. sugar • 1 oz. yeast
1 gallon water

Crush the currants and leave to soak overnight. Boil the water and when it has cooled a little pour it over the fruit. Leave to soak for twelve hours and then strain through fine muslin. Put the strained juice through a jelly-bag and let it drain. Bring the juice just to boiling-point and simmer gently for three minutes. Then pour the hot juice over the sugar in the fermenting vessel and stir until all the sugar is dissolved. Allow the brew to cool, sprinkle the yeast on top and stir in. Cover up and ferment for fourteen days; then proceed with bottling.

Cherry Wine

(using black cherries)

6 lb. cherries • 4½ lb. sugar • 1 gallon water
1 oz. yeast

Crush the cherries without breaking the stones and then pour the boiling water over them. Leave to soak for forty-eight hours. Strain through fine muslin and then put the juice through a jelly-bag. Bring the juice just to boiling-point and pour it over the sugar. Stir until the sugar is dissolved. Allow to cool and then sprinkle the yeast on top and stir in. Cover as directed and ferment for fourteen days; after which proceed with bottling.

Mulberry Wine

4 lb. mulberries • 4 lb. sugar • 1 gallon water
1 oz. yeast

Crush the mulberries and pour the boiling water over them. Leave to soak for twenty-four hours and then strain the pulp through a jelly-bag. Bring the juice just to boiling-point and then pour it over the sugar. Stir until the sugar is dissolved. Allow to cool and then sprinkle the yeast on top and stir in. Cover as directed and ferment for fourteen days; after which proceed with bottling.

Apricot Wine

(using fresh fruit)
5 lb. apricots (weighed with the stones)
4 lb. sugar • 1 gallon water • 1 oz. yeast

Halve the apricots and pour the boiling water over them. As soon as the water is cool enough, crush the fruits well by hand and then leave to soak for forty-eight hours. Crush well again, strain through muslin and put the juice through a jelly-bag. Bring the juice to boiling-point and simmer for ten minutes. Pour the hot juice over the sugar and stir until all the sugar is dissolved. Allow to cool and then sprinkle the yeast on top and stir in. Cover as directed and ferment for fourteen days; then proceed with bottling.

APPLE WINE

(as distinct from cider)

6 lb. good-quality juicy apples (if slightly bruised cut out the bruised parts)
1 lb. raisins • 4 lb. sugar • 1 oz. yeast
1 gallon water

Wipe the apples clean with a damp cloth and then grate them, discarding the cores. Put the grated apples in the water and soak for forty-eight hours. Stir well occasionally and then crush with the hands and strain through fine muslin. Put the juice through a jelly-bag. Bring the juice just to boiling-point and simmer for five minutes. Pour the hot liquid over the sugar and stir until all the sugar is dissolved. Then put in the cut-up raisins. When it has cooled, sprinkle the yeast on top and stir in. Cover as directed and ferment for fourteen days; after which, strain and proceed with bottling.

QUINCE WINE

Quince is a fruit which at one time could be found in most cottage gardens. Excellent jams and jellies are made from quinces – also delicious wine. I haven't seen a quince for years; they are a hard pear-shaped fruit with a skin like flannel, and are dry to the palate.

4 lb. quinces • 4½ lb. sugar • rinds of 3 lemons
1 oz. yeast • 1 gallon water

Wipe the fruit clean with a damp cloth and then grate them, discarding the cores. Pour the boiling water over the grated fruit and leave to soak for forty-eight hours. Stir well occasionally and then crush with the hands, and strain through fine muslin. Strain the juice through a jelly-bag. Bring the juice to boiling-point and simmer for five minutes. Pour the hot liquid over the sugar and stir until the sugar is dissolved. Then grate the lemon rinds into the brew. Allow the brew to cool and then sprinkle the yeast on top and stir in. Cover as directed and ferment for fourteen days; then strain and proceed with bottling.

Damson and Apple Wine

2½ lb. juicy apples (any sweet variety will do)
2½ lb. damsons (weighed with the stones)
3½ lb. sugar • 1 oz. yeast • 9 pints water

Wipe the apples clean with a damp cloth and then grate them, discarding the cores. Crush the damsons and put the fruits together. Pour the cold water over them and leave to soak for forty-eight hours. Stir occasionally and then crush well and strain through fine muslin. Strain the juice through a jelly-bag. Bring the strained juice to boiling-point and boil gently for three minutes. Pour the hot liquid over the sugar and stir until all the sugar is dissolved. When the brew has cooled, sprinkle the yeast on top and stir in. Cover as directed and ferment for fourteen days; then proceed with bottling.

Lemon Wine

6 medium-sized lemons • ½ lb. raisins
4 lb. sugar • 1 oz. yeast • 1 gallon water

(*Note:* eight or even ten lemons may be used if you like very strong flavours.)

Halve the lemons and squeeze the juice into one gallon of boiling water, and when the water boils again cut off the heat at once. Pour the hot liquid over the sugar and stir until all the sugar is dissolved. Cut up the raisins and add these to the liquid. Then grate the lemon rinds into the brew. Allow the brew to cool and then sprinkle the yeast on top and stir in. Cover as directed and ferment for fourteen days; after which, strain and proceed with bottling.

Grapefruit Wine

6 grapefruit • 1 lb. raisins • 4 lb. sugar
1 oz. yeast • 1 gallon water

Halve the grapefruit and squeeze the juice into the boiling water, and when the water boils again cut off the heat at once. Pour the hot liquid over the sugar and stir until all the sugar is dissolved. Then add the cut-up raisins. Allow the brew to cool and then sprinkle the yeast on top and stir in. Cover as directed and ferment for fourteen days; after which strain and proceed with bottling.

Loganberry Wine

3 pints loganberries • 3½ lb. sugar
1 oz. yeast • 1 gallon water

Crush the fruits and pour the boiling water over them. Allow to soak overnight, stirring occasionally. Then crush well, strain through muslin and put the juice through a jelly-bag. Bring the strained juice just to boiling-point and simmer for three minutes. Pour the hot juice over the sugar and stir until all the sugar is dissolved. Allow the brew to cool and then sprinkle the yeast on top and stir in. Cover as directed and ferment for fourteen days; after which proceed with bottling.

Raspberry Wine

4 lb. raspberries • 3½ lb. sugar • 1 oz. yeast
1 gallon water

Crush the raspberries, pour the boiling water over them and leave to soak for forty-eight hours. Stir, crush well with the hands and then strain the pulp through a jelly-bag. Bring the juice just to boiling-point and simmer for two minutes. Pour the hot liquid over the sugar and stir until all the sugar is dissolved. Allow the brew to cool and then sprinkle the yeast on top and stir in. Cover as directed and ferment for fourteen days; then proceed with bottling.

Blackberry Wine

4½ lb. blackberries • 4½ lb. sugar • 1 oz. yeast
1 gallon water

Crush the blackberries, pour them into the boiling water and cut off the heat at once. While the pulp is still hot, strain through fine muslin and then put the juice through a jelly-bag. Bring the strained juice to boiling-point and simmer for two minutes. Pour the hot liquid over the sugar and stir until all the sugar is dissolved. Allow the brew to cool, sprinkle the yeast on top, and stir in. Cover as directed and ferment for fourteen days; then proceed with bottling.

Pear Wine

5 lb. pears • 2 oranges • 2 lemons
4 lb. sugar • 1 oz. yeast • 1 gallon water

Almost any kind of pear will do for this wine: the little hard ones that children like to get their teeth into or the large hard cooking pears. If a medium-sweet variety is used, take three-and-a-half pounds sugar; if very sweet, use three pounds.

Wipe the pears clean with a damp cloth and remove the doubtful parts, then grate them, discarding the cores, and pour the boiling water over them. Allow the mixture to soak for forty-eight hours and then crush the fruit as much as you can. Strain through muslin and put the juice through a jelly-bag. Bring the strained juice just to boiling-point and simmer for three minutes. Pour the hot liquid over the sugar and stir until all the sugar is dissolved. Then halve the lemons and oranges and squeeze the juice into the brew. Allow the brew to cool, sprinkle the yeast on top and stir in. Cover it up and ferment for fourteen days; after which, proceed with bottling.

Orange Wine

12 large, 15 medium or 20 small oranges
4 lb. sugar • 1 oz. yeast • 1 gallon water

Wipe the oranges clean with a damp cloth and cut them into small pieces. Pour the boiling water over them and leave to soak for two days. Crush well each day and work the peel between the fingers to extract the oil – doubling the peel over and pressing well (much flavour is obtained from this). Strain, and put the juice through a jelly-bag, warming the juice to assist the sugar to dissolve. Stir until all the sugar is dissolved, and when the brew is cool enough sprinkle the yeast on top and stir in. Cover as directed and ferment for fourteen days; after which, proceed with bottling.

Tangerine Special

12–15 tangerines • 3½ lb. sugar • 1 oz. yeast
1 gallon water

Peel the tangerines and crush them by hand. Discard the peels. Pour the boiling water over the crushed fruit, and leave to soak for twelve hours. Strain and warm the juice to assist the sugar to dissolve. Pour the juice over the sugar and stir until all the sugar is dissolved. When the brew is cool enough sprinkle the yeast on top and stir in. Cover as directed and ferment for fourteen days; after which, proceed with bottling.

For Your Own Recipes

For Your Own Recipes

6

Sherry

The flavour of commercial sherry is obtained from a bacterial growth called *flor*, the secret of which is jealously guarded by the sherry producers of Spain. So we cannot give our home-made sherry that unmistakable flavour; nevertheless, the following recipes will produce good imitations of that much-blended, much fortified wine.

These sherries are neither sweet nor dry: they are designed to suit the average palate. If you like your sherry very dry, use only two pounds of sugar. If you prefer it fairly dry, use three pounds of sugar. If your palate for sherry is 'just ordinary', follow the recipes to the letter.

SHERRY

2 lb. very oldest potatoes • ½ lb. raisins
4 lb. sugar • 2 lb. green or amber grapes
1 oz. bruised ginger • 1 oz. yeast
5 quarts water

Do not peel the potatoes, but scrub them thoroughly and then grate. Put them in the water, bring slowly to boiling-point and simmer for not more than ten minutes, taking off all the scum that rises. Strain into the fermenting vessel and pour in the sugar at once. Stir until all the sugar is dissolved and then add the chopped raisins and bruised ginger. Then crush the grapes into a bowl and strain the juice into the potato water. Allow the brew to cool, sprinkle the yeast on top and stir in. After fourteen days' fermentation strain and proceed with isinglass and bottling.

Sherry

2 lb. very oldest potatoes · 1½ lb. green grapes
1 lb. raisins · ½ lb. wheat · juice of 1 large grapefruit
1 oz. bruised ginger · 3½ lb. sugar
1 oz. yeast · 5 quarts water

Do not peel the potatoes, but scrub them thoroughly and then grate them. Put them in the water and bring them slowly to boiling-point. Simmer gently for not more than ten minutes, taking off all the scum that rises. Strain into the fermenting vessel and add the sugar at once. Stir until all the sugar is dissolved and then add the chopped raisins and bruised ginger. Crush the grapes and add the juice and the skins to the potato water; then add the wheat. Allow it to cool and then sprinkle the yeast on top and stir it in. After fourteen days' fermentation, strain and proceed with isinglass and bottling.

Sherry

2¼ lb. very oldest parsnips
2 lb. green grapes that are inclined to be on the 'sharp' side – or little outdoor-grown grapes will do
¼ lb. raisins · ¼ lb. sultanas
½ oz. bruised ginger · 3½ lb. sugar · 1 oz. yeast
5 quarts water

Scrub the parsnips clean, grate them and put them in the water. Bring slowly to boiling-point and simmer for not more than ten minutes. Strain at once, add the sugar and stir until dissolved. Crush the grapes and strain them and add this juice to the parsnip water. Then add the chopped raisins, chopped sultanas and bruised ginger. Allow the brew to cool and then sprinkle the yeast on top and stir in. After fourteen days' fermentation, strain and then proceed with isinglass and bottling.

7

Dried-fruit Wines

Raisin Wine

3 lb. raisins • 2 oranges • 2 lemons
2½ lb. sugar • 1 oz. yeast • 9 pints water

Chop the raisins and pour the boiling water over them. Leave to soak for forty-eight hours, stirring occasionally. Then crush well with the hands and strain. Into this liquid squeeze the oranges and lemons and bring the whole liquid just to boiling-point. Pour this over the sugar and stir until all the sugar is dissolved.

Allow it to cool and then sprinkle the yeast on top and stir in. After fourteen days' fermentation, proceed with isinglass and bottling.

Currant Wine

2½ lb. currants • 2 grapefruit • 3 lb. sugar
1 oz. yeast • 9 pints water

Bring the water just to boiling-point and pour in the currants. Cut off the heat at once. Leave the mixture to soak for forty-eight hours, stirring occasionally. Then crush well with the hands and strain. Into this strained liquid squeeze the grapefruit and then bring the liquid just to boiling-point and simmer for three minutes. Pour the hot liquid over the sugar and stir until all the sugar is dissolved. When the brew is cool, sprinkle the yeast on top and stir in. Allow it to ferment for fourteen days and proceed with isinglass and bottling.

Dried-Fruit Wines

Prune Wine

3 lb. dried prunes • ½ lb. sultanas
2 grapefruit • 3 lb. sugar • 1 oz. yeast
9 pints water

Cut the prunes down one side, stone them, and put them in the boiling water. Cut off the heat at once. Allow the mixture to soak overnight, and then crush well with the hands and strain. Into this strained liquid squeeze the grapefruit. Bring the liquid to boiling-point and simmer for two or three minutes – no longer. Pour the hot liquid over the sugar and stir until all the sugar is dissolved. Add the chopped sultanas to this liquid, and allow it to cool. Then sprinkle the yeast on top and stir in. After fourteen days' fermentation, strain and proceed with isinglass and bottling.

Dried-Apricot Wine

4 lb. dried apricots
8 almonds (which should be shredded)
3½ lb. sugar • 1 oz. yeast • 9 pints water

Bring the water to boiling-point and pour in the apricots. Cut off the heat at once and allow the mixture to soak for forty-eight hours, stirring occasionally. Then crush well with the hands and strain. Into this liquid put the almonds and bring to the boil, boiling gently for two minutes. Pour the hot liquid over the sugar and stir until all the sugar is dissolved. Allow the brew to cool and then sprinkle the yeast on top and stir in. After fourteen days' fermentation proceed with isinglass and bottling.

MIXED DRIED-FRUIT WINES

Many excellent wines can be made from a mixture of dried fruits, and the method used is the same in each case.

Date Wine

2½ lb. packeted dates or those sold by weight
2 oranges • 2 lemons • 2 cloves
3 lb. sugar • 1 oz. yeast • 9 pints water

Bring the water to boiling-point and put in the finely cut-up dates. Cut off the heat at once. Leave to soak for forty-eight hours and then strain. Into this strained liquid squeeze the lemons and oranges. Bring the liquid to boiling-point and simmer for three minutes. Pour the hot liquid over the sugar and stir until all the sugar is dissolved. Allow the brew to cool, sprinkle the yeast on top and stir in. Then add the cloves and put the orange and lemon rinds into the brew, leaving them to float during the fermentation period. After fourteen days' fermentation, strain and proceed with isinglass and bottling.

In the following five recipes the method used is the same as that given above for Date Wine.

Raisin, Prune and Sultana Wine

1 lb. prunes • 1 lb. raisins • ½ lb. sultanas
2¼ lb. sugar • 1 oz. yeast • 9 pints water

Proceed as for Date Wine, above.

Currant, Sultana and Prune Wine

1 lb. currants • 1 lb. sultanas • ½ lb. prunes
2 oranges • 2 lemons • 3 lb. sugar
1 oz. yeast • 9 pints water

Proceed as for Date Wine, above.

Date, Prune and Fig Wine

1 lb. dates • 1 lb. prunes • 1 lb. figs
2 oranges and 2 grapefruit
(or 3 grapefruit and no oranges)
3 lb. sugar • 1 oz. yeast • 9 pints water
Proceed as for Date Wine, page 66.

Apricot, Prune and Sultana Wine

1½ lb. apricots • 1½ lb. prunes • ½ lb. sultanas
2 oranges • 2 lemons • 3 lb. sugar
1 oz. yeast • 9 pints water
Proceed as for Date Wine, page 66.

Fig Wine

Bear in mind that this wine has laxative properties. It is probably the only alcoholic laxative there is.

2½ lb. figs • 2 grapefruit (or 3 lemons)
½ oz. bruised ginger • 3 lb. sugar
1 oz. yeast • 9 pints water
Proceed as for Date Wine, page 66.

For Your Own Recipes

For Your Own Recipes

8
Flower and Sugar Wines

These flower wines clear very readily without the use of isinglass; they are usually high in proof spirit, and their flavours are delicately aromatic.

Clover Wine (mauve)

3 quarts clover heads • 1 grapefruit
3½ lb. sugar • 1 oz. yeast • 1 gallon water

When the flowers have been gathered, pull off the petals – they will all come easily if you hold the petals in one hand and the base of the flower head in the other.

Bring the water to boiling-point and pour in the flowers. Cut off the heat at once and allow to soak for four days. Strain and warm the juice enough to help the sugar dissolve. Stir in the sugar and when all is dissolved add the yeast. Cut the grapefruit into slices and float them on the surface of the brew. Cover as directed and ferment for fourteen days; then strain or take off the floating fruit and proceed with bottling.

Coltsfoot Wine

1 gallon coltsfoot flowers • 3½ lb. sugar
1 oz. yeast • 1 gallon water

When the flowers have been gathered pull off the petals – these, like clover, will come quite easily if the petals are held in one hand and the base of the flower head in the other. Pour the boiling water over the petals and allow to soak for three days. Strain, bring the liquid just to boiling-point and add the sugar at once. Stir until the sugar is dissolved. Allow the brew to cool and then sprinkle the yeast on top and stir in. Cover as directed and ferment for fourteen days; after which proceed with bottling.

Dandelion Wine

Dandelion wine lays claim to many tonic properties, one being that it tones up the liver. It is also said to be partly responsible for the longevity of gipsies. Gather the flowers on a sunny day when they are fully open: closed, they teem with insects which would emerge during soaking and one might get dandelion-cum-insect-juice wine.

1 gallon flower heads
with not the tiniest piece of stalk
3 lb. sugar • 1 oz. yeast • 9 pints water

Petals only should be used, but you can use the whole heads if you wish. Pour the boiling water over the flower heads (or petals) and leave to soak for five days, stirring well each day. If mould begins to form on the surface scoop it off. Keep well covered up. After five days' soaking, strain and warm the juice to help the sugar dissolve. Pour the liquid over the sugar and stir until all the sugar is dissolved. When the brew is cool enough, sprinkle the yeast on top and stir in. Cover as directed and ferment for fourteen days; after which proceed with bottling.

Sugar Wine

3 lb. sugar • 1 oz. yeast • 1 gallon water

Bring the water to boiling-point and pour in the sugar; keep stirring until all the sugar is dissolved and then let the water reach boiling-point again. Cut off the heat at once. Allow the brew to cool and then sprinkle the yeast on top and stir in. Cover as directed.

When fermentation has been going on for forty-eight hours, add the flowers of your choice to flavour the brew. You can use:

Hawthorn blossom	2 pints
Elder-flowers	2 pints
Primroses	3 pints
Rose petals	2–3 pints as available
Cowslips	3 pints
Marigolds (not the African variety: petals only)	3 pints
Wallflowers (petals only)	3 pints

Having added your choice of flowers, stir well in and allow fermentation to proceed for the full fourteen days' period. Then strain, and proceed with bottling.

Multi-Flavoured Sugar Wine

This recipe will prove useful if, for lack of space or other reasons, you can only make small quantities. The recipe is designed for one gallon of wine, but there is nothing to prevent anyone making half that amount merely by using half the amounts of ingredients listed. An old friend of mine makes a quart at a time – using a tiny cupboard beside the fire as the warm place for fermenting the brew. She has a weakness for gin, which is beyond her pension, but by using a quarter-bottle of gin and diluting it with sugar wine, she does very nicely.

3 lb. sugar • 1 oz. yeast • 9 pints water

Bring the water to boiling-point and pour in the sugar. Cut off the heat and stir until the sugar is dissolved. Allow the liquid to cool and then sprinkle the yeast on top and stir in. Cover as directed and ferment for fourteen days; after which, bottle as usual and treat as any other wine.

When the wine is perfectly clear, siphon the clear

wine off any lees that may happen to be there, and put into sterilized bottles. Before sealing them, the flavouring medium of your choice may be added. Try mint, peppermint, ginger, coffee – the variety of flavourings that may be added is limited only by your own imagination and taste. I cannot imagine anything more surprising than alcoholic coffee – try it on your friends. You can, of course, flavour it by diluting (as my old friend does) with gin – or whisky or brandy. In any case, different flavourings may be used for each glass of wine taken from the bottle. In this event no flavouring at all should be added until one wishes to use the wine.

ELDER-FLOWER CHAMPAGNE
(non-alcoholic)

This is a refreshing summer drink.

1 quart elder-flowers stripped from the stalks when in full bloom
2 oranges • 2 lemons
3 dessertspoonfuls of white or wine vinegar
1 lb sugar • 1 gallon water

Cut the fruit into slices, put them in the water and bring just to boiling-point. Cut off the heat, allow the mixture to cool and then add the elder-flowers, stirring them in. Leave to soak for forty-eight hours and then strain through very fine muslin. Pour the strained liquid over the sugar and stir until all is dissolved. Then add the vinegar. Bottle, and cork well.

This should keep for a month or so. It is delicious served with ice.

Hawthorn blossom may be used in place of elder-flowers.

For Your Own Recipes

For Your Own Recipes

9
Mixed Drinks for the Party

Hot Punch

3 pints of old ale or good-quality beer
(not bottled ale)
1 pint home-made wine (orange, lemon, grapefruit or strongly-flavoured root-wine is best)
1 sliced lemon · pinch of ginger · 1 clove

Bring the ale or beer to boiling-point and cut off the heat at once. Pour in the wine and then add the ginger and clove. Use the sliced lemon only if lemon wine has not been used – squeeze it into the mixture and leave the slices floating while you keep the brew hot on a low gas for five minutes. Strain and serve hot.

This punch cannot be stored: make it in smaller quantities, or as desired.

Mint-Julep

½ pint light ale · ¼ pint water
1 double glass home-made or commercial sherry
juice of 1 lemon · 2 fresh mint leaves

Mix the liquids together and sweeten to taste. Add the juice of the lemon and then bruise the mint leaves and float them on the surface for ten minutes. Stir well, take off the mint leaves and serve.

Tea Wine

Make a pot of tea and let it stand for five minutes. Strain into a jug, and to each cupful of tea add 1½ teaspoonfuls of sugar. Then add 1 wine-glassful of strongly-flavoured home-made wine (not port-style) to each cup of tea. Serve warm or cold.

Imitation Sherry Cobbler

½ pint home-made or commercial sherry
2 wine-glassfuls orange wine or orange juice
juice of ½ lemon

Squeeze the lemon into the sherry and mix the ingredients together. Sweeten to taste, and serve.

Imitation Egg Flip

White of 1 egg • 1 cupful milk
3 dessertspoonfuls home-made sherry (other home-made wines, not port-style, may be used)

Mix the milk with the sherry by stirring briskly with a fork. Whisk the egg-white until it is stiff and frothy. Then pour this into the milk-sherry mixture and whisk well. Serve after five minutes.

Ginger Beer (alcoholic)

As we all know, ginger beer should be cloudy, and this characteristic is produced by boiling the ingredients (including the ginger) in the water. Ginger beer is subject to licensing laws: it must not be made to a greater strength than 2 per cent of proof spirit.

Made in the following manner and with the exact amount of sugar prescribed, the beer will be within the permitted maximum. Naturally, ginger beer has to be 'fizzing'; I can hardly call it 'sparkling' because it also has to be cloudy. In view of this you will appreciate that some skill is needed to make it properly.

2 oz. bruised Jamaican ginger • 3 lemons
1 oz. cream of tartar • ¼ oz. citric acid
2 gallons water • 1½ lb. sugar • 1 oz. yeast

Slice the lemons and put them into a large china jug with other ingredients. Pour the boiling water over them. Now put the jug into a large saucepan partly filled with water and boil for ten minutes, stirring the contents of the jug several times. Boil the remainder of the two gallons of water and put this into the fermenting vessel. Then pour the jug of ingredients into this. Leave overnight. Strain, and add one ounce of yeast. When the beer has been fermenting for eight or twelve hours it should be safe to bottle it and screw home the stoppers. Strain before bottling, of course, and if fermentation seems to be rather too vigorous, leave for a little while before screwing home the stoppers.

As with brewing beers and ales (see next chapter), the skill comes in deciding the exact moment to screw up.

10

Cider, Ale, Beer and Stout

As a child I well remember the travelling cider press that clanked to a standstill at the gate of my grandparents' cottage. Its arrival was anticipated weeks ahead and most people had their apples ready, with the barrels and other things needed for the job of converting the apple into the drink of the countryman. I was too young to be able to remember all the details of those days, but I can recall that my grandfather used to commandeer every local child, not already employed by its parents, to help collect the apples, and woe betide any of them that ate an apple before the job was finished.

In a good year – as my parents have told me since – my grandfather would turn out as much as a hundred gallons of the best cider in the district. And nearly all of it, they maintained, he drank himself.

He used about fifteen hundredweight of apples of different varieties 'all shoved in together', and heaven knows how much sugar. If he used as much per gallon as we do at present for making wine, then it was hardly cider he made, but rather apple wine. No wonder his cider was known to be the best; for 'best' to the countryman's reckoning is the smallest amount that can knock a man off his feet. My father swore that there was not a man living – and they could drink in those days – who could drink a quart of grandad's cider and get home under his own steam.

I have never made cider, because I have never had the space to do it, and have been far too busy with winemaking. And, unfortunately, the recipe handed on to my parents was lost during the war together with a lot of other valuable recipes.

However, I have here a recipe which, I am assured by a friend, the one who collects rain-water, will make cider as good as the best. Experienced wine-makers will have no trouble with this method.

He maintains that, strictly speaking, there is no right or wrong way about amateur cider-making. Each home operator favours a slightly different method and each makes a good job of cider-brewing, while maintaining that his own method is the best. They use whichever apples happen to be available, not necessarily those that give the best results – usually a mixture of varieties that often includes too many sweet ones or too many of a 'sharp' variety. Nevertheless, they all turn out a really good drop of stuff to satisfy both their own personal taste and that of their friends.

My friend uses a press which belongs to a group who run their own cider-making circle; this spreads the expense of both press and barrels over a number of users.

To make seven gallons of 'still' cider he uses one hundredweight of apples, the sweetest and juiciest he can get.

After pressing, the juice is put into a sulphured tub and three pounds of sugar are added to every gallon of juice. This is stirred until it is dissolved and then eight ounces of yeast are stirred in. The liquid is kept in a fairly warm atmosphere so that fermentation gets under way without delay.

After seven days' fermentation he samples the cider daily. When he is satisfied with the flavour and the alcohol content (which he judges by taste) he stops fermentation by adding sulphur-dioxide tablets. Three to each gallon is usually enough, but sometimes, especially if the weather happens to be warm for the season (the cider is usually made at the end of September or early October), one more may be needed.

If fermentation is allowed to carry itself to a natural conclusion the cider might well be anything up to 14 per cent alcohol by volume and therefore too strong to be drunk by the pint – or even the half-pint. By arresting fermentation when the cider tastes 'right' he gets exactly what he wants.

When fermentation has ceased he puts the cider into stone jars and leaves it undisturbed for three months. By that time it is crystal-clear. When this stage is reached the cider is bottled and used as required.

To make a *sparkling* cider one would have to follow the directions given for making champagne on page 153.

For a *dry* cider, much less sugar is needed and fermentation is arrested when the required degree of sweetness has been reached. This is determined by daily sampling. If a very dry and very strong cider is required, add, say, two pounds of sugar to each gallon of juice and allow fermentation to carry on to its natural conclusion. The cider will not necessarily be as strong as 14 per cent because fermentation ceases when there is no more sugar to be converted into alcohol.

If the cider turns out too dry and sweetening is necessary, this has to be done with sugar or golden syrup when the finished cider has become crystal-clear and has been siphoned into bottles.

Space is left in each bottle and some cider is made into a sweet syrup with sugar or golden syrup. This is then added to each bottle, and the bottles corked as soon as possible.

Care must be taken here, because if any 'live' yeast spores are present in the cider, the sweetening medium will give rise to further fermentation within the bottles. This need not result in a series of explosions: the added sugar might well be used up before the pressure inside the bottles became too great; it would mean that you would have a medium-dry sparkling cider, whether you liked it or not.

Don't throw away the apple-pulp from the press for this may be made into a delicious *Spiced Apple Wine* by using the following method.

Measure the pulp, and to each gallon add one quart of water and one pound of sugar. The sugar will have to be dissolved in warmed water before it is added to the pulp. To each gallon of this mixture add half a pound of raisins, half a pound of kibbled maize and two cloves. Then add the yeast, and proceed as you would with any other kind of wine.

Ales, Beers and Stouts

There is no need here for lengthy details of the brewing of ales and beers, for packets of dried malt and hops, and jars of concentrated extract of malt and hops, are readily obtainable from firms dealing in wine-makers' and home-brewers' requirements; and these are invariably accompanied by the fullest directions for brewing. The following, however, should be borne in mind.

All fermenting liquors are open to attacks by acetic bacteria and wild yeasts (see 'The Enemies', page 6). Home brewers of beers and stouts, therefore, must take the same precautions against these micro-organisms as home wine-makers do.

The risk of contamination when brewing beers, etc., is considerably lessened by the short period of fermentation – two or three days – and if the fermenting beers are covered in the same way as fermenting wines, they should be quite safe.

The greatest risk of contamination comes from utensils, bottles, etc. Home brewers must sterilize *all* utensils either chemically or by boiling, as I have explained for home wine-making.

Wooden fermenting vessels and closed casks – those in which the beer is kept – must be sterilized by having sulphur burned inside them. This is not an easy thing to do in a small space, so if you live in a flat it might be best to use only stone jars and stone fermenting vessels. Wooden casks, etc., must not be sterilized with liquid sulphur; the wood absorbs this and not only would the subsequent brew be ruined by the flavour of the sulphur, but it is most unlikely that the brew would ferment at all, for excess sulphur will destroy the yeast organism.

Wooden casks and such-like may be effectively sterilized with a small piece of sulphur burning in a large spoon. The spoon should be attached to a cane and then led into the cask. And this job should be done out of doors.

I strongly advise all those interested in taking up home brewing to use stone fermenting vessels – those fitted with taps are best, for they allow the lees to settle below the level of the tap itself and the moderately clear beer may then be drawn off without disturbing the lees.

If a two-way tap is available, so much the better. This means that the tap can be turned to fill one bottle, and then switched to fill the next, which is held in readiness. By this means sudden stoppage of flow is avoided and there is no churning up of the lees, which so often takes place when the flow is suddenly halted. If you have ever siphoned wine off lees in a glass jar you will know how important continuous flow really is.

The skill in home brewing comes in deciding the best time to cork the bottles. And this each operator must decide for himself. Screw-stoppers are used, of course, and they must be screwed home when you have decided that fermentation is nearly over. Fermentation must continue long enough to charge the beer with sufficient carbon dioxide to put a head on top of your glass, but at the same time not so long that the bottles explode. The risk of this is so slight that it may almost be disregarded, for the amount of sugar added can only ferment for a certain time (depending on temperature), and by the time you have made, say, three brews, you will be quite able to decide the exact moment for screwing home the stoppers. You may cork too late the first time, with the result that the beer is a bit flat. Next time, you may screw home the stoppers too soon, with the result that when you unscrew them you have beer all over the ceiling. But you will find it surprisingly easy next time to decide the exact moment for screwing up.

Packeted malt and dried hops sufficient to make four gallons of brew cost about three shillings or three and sixpence. And it will make a drink equal to that costing one and threepence a pint in your local. As it is so cheap, the possible loss of the first brew will not be a calamity.

The amount of sugar prescribed in the recipes provided by the supplier will produce a brew containing 2 per cent of proof spirit, and you can make all you like at this strength without a brewer's licence. To be on the safe side, call your brews 'home-brew' and not by the proper name – 'ale', 'beer', 'stout', or whichever you are making.

You must not sell your home-brew and you must not make it stronger than 2 per cent (it is quite a simple matter to do so) without a licence: if you do, and the local excise people find out, it might cost you as much as fifty pounds in fines.

The risk of contamination by acetic bacteria and other of the enemies of successful wine-making and home brewing – slight though it is – is completely eliminated by the use of fermentation locks (see page 91). These also help to retain the carbon-dioxide gas so important to beers, and help the brewer to control the progress of fermentation.

This is all that need be said of home brewing, apart from adding that the home brewing of beers, etc., is undergoing a revival in this country and on the other side of the Atlantic. The export of British malt and hops – the best in the world – is a dollar-earner, and purchase in ready made-up quantities has advantages over the buying of loose lots and working it all out for oneself.

The beginner would do well to divide the first four-gallon packet he buys into lots sufficient to make four separate gallons: by the time you have used up the whole packet you will be quite experienced. If you do this, remember to use only a quarter of the amount of sugar prescribed in the recipe supplied with the packet of ingredients.

My grandfather, an estate blacksmith in the 'spreading chestnut tree' style, was a barrel-bellied block of a man with an immense capacity for good beer. He swore that there was no beer to compare with the stuff he could turn out in a converted pig-sty at the end of his orchard. If regulations controlling the strength of home-brews were the same in those days as they are today, then I am afraid he must have sailed pretty close to the wind. For, young as I was at the time, I well remember hearing how any unsuspecting visitor taking more than one pint invariably finished up under the table.

And I can remember it being said that my grandmother could barter a bottle of wine for anything we wanted, from a chicken to a bushel of malt. She was famous locally for her wine; every visitor was regaled with it. And I recall how, sitting in her high-backed stump-leg wooden chair, she would listen to and agree with everything the vicar had to say of the evils of alcohol. I often wonder what would have happened had she had to answer the door while he was there, for invariably, under her chair, hidden by the austere folds of her ankle-length black skirt, was a bottle of her best.

Both my grandparents lived to be over eighty, so there can be little wrong with home-made wines and beers.

11

If You Experiment

Vegetable wine, fruit wine, flower wine – there are hundreds of recipes, all different yet all basically the same; and if you like to experiment there is a vast field in which to do so. If you consider the sherry recipes as examples of fruit and vegetable mixtures for the purpose of making delicious wines, you will see at once that experiment is worth while.

During the last war, when sugar for wine-making was unobtainable, tinned syrup and 'sugar' obtained by boiling packet dates with the little real sugar I did happen to acquire, helped to keep my little brewery working, if only to the extent of half a dozen gallons a year. The wine was not nearly as good as that turned out today, but cheer was hard to come by and anything reasonably good was better than nothing at all.

Since the war, and especially since the de-rationing of sugar, experimenting with various recipes has been my hobby. The result of one such experiment, with a strongly-flavoured orange wine and mildly-flavoured potato wine, I at once called orange brandy. However, I thought that to make two varieties of wine in order to produce one really good one seemed an odd way of doing the job, so I studied both recipes and then set to work. The result, which really was wonderful, I called Bravery's Extra-Special Fine Old Jungle-Juice (see page 27). Thus experimenting with two recipes and two varieties of wine proved not only the worth of experiment, but also the value of blending.

Readers following any of the hundred-odd recipes in this book, bearing in mind all I have said about the best ingredients, sterilisation of utensils, fermentation, the removal of scum during simmering, and the clearing process, will turn out really magnificent wines. Nevertheless there are many recipes waiting to be discovered.

Therefore I say, 'Experiment'. For who knows what might turn up quite accidentally?

I have proved that what appears to be a good idea is usually worth following up. So when you have had a little experience, and are turning out rich, crystal-clear wines with professional regularity, and when you have mastered the technique of blending – if you try this – many ideas for recipes will occur to you. Try them out in half-gallon lots and when you have turned out something really good of your own, test it on your friends. Then work the recipe once more, taking careful note of all you do. When you have perfected a recipe – but not before – pass it on.

Many people jealously guard secrets which should be handed on. Typical is the case of a late friend of mine who, with the aid of his three sons, brewed stout each year from elderberries.

Many's the time I have tried to winkle the recipe out of him, but a sly wink and the up-ending of his glass was his only response. Since I enjoyed his stout so much I thought it wise not to be too inquisitive. Imagine my surprise when, after his death, the lads explained that all they had been allowed to do was collect the elderberries and help to crush them. After which the cunning old devil – as they affectionately called him – brewed his stout behind locked doors. Search as we might, neither recipe nor notes did we find.

Knowledge gained from years of experiment both with recipe and method was all kept in his head, and he took it with him.

Blending

Blending, which also offers wide scope to those of an experimental turn of mind, may result in blends or cocktails to surpass even one's wildest hopes.

First, do not blend wines that have not yet matured, for although you may get the required flavour at the time of blending, the flavour and bouquet of each wine used will have altered considerably by the time each wine in the blend has reached maturity.

Second, do not splosh bottles of two or three varieties of wine into each other and expect a miracle to happen. Approach the job seriously – it is well worth while. Familiarize yourself with the flavour of each wine to be used in the blend and then decide which you wish to predominate when blending is completed: this would be the basic brew – as gin is the basis of most cocktails. To half a tumbler of your basic brew add your other wines with a teaspoon; carefully does it. Take the merest sip after each wine has been added, and when you are satisfied, the blending may be done on a larger scale; say, one bottle of this, half a bottle of that and a quarter-bottle of what have you. Keep notes as each teaspoonful of wine is added to the basic brew.

As an example we have, say, a strongly-flavoured grapefruit wine: to this may be added various root wines which you think may be improved by blending. While blending take a little cheese between each sip: this will clear the palate so that the slight difference – which would otherwise be unnoticeable – immediately becomes apparent.

Cheese may also be taken when tasting different bottles of one variety of wine made with varied amounts of the same ingredients.

All blended wine should be kept for at least six months to allow for the 'marrying' of the wines in the blend. Here are some suggestions for blending the port-style wines:

Elderberry, damson and blackcurrant
Victoria plum, dried prune and blackcurrant
Damson, blackberry and elderberry
Victoria plum, blackberry and elderberry

Doubtless many variations of the above will now occur to you. Three wines are not always needed; two are often sufficient.

12

Wine-making and the Law

When you are, as you surely will be, turning out gallon upon gallon of delicious, crystal-clear wines, and when you have mastered the technique of blending (if you want to), and have experimented a little of your own accord, you may, like many other people, try to make your wine even better.

The idea of distilling home-made wines occurs to most people at some time or other and, fortunately, the idea dies as quickly as it is conceived. A few people, however, do try tampering with the stuff: and it is to these tempted few that this warning is directed.

Violence, insanity, blindness and even murder have resulted through drinking distilled home-made wine. In the mining and construction camps of Prohibition America, the easy-money boys set up stills in which harmless brews were turned into rot-gut liquor. Gangers and construction managers, worried by accidents and absenteeism, tried at first to handle the situation themselves, but the trade quickly got out of hand. Men normally of sound mind and judgment became killers at the flick of a card; spirit-inflamed suspicion sent them berserk with knives, guns or whatever came to hand. Permanent blindness struck down many, while others died of alcoholic poisoning.

So be warned, you tempted few: home distilling, besides carrying heavy penalties, is a very dangerous practice. Leave it alone – be satisfied.

Apart from the heavy penalties for illegal distilling (which may under certain circumstances amount to a fine of one hundred pounds or even more, with imprisonment for a second conviction), the risk of injury to health through drinking the raw spirit should be enough to deter even the most adventurous.

Spirit distilled in the home is very greatly overproof – the amount depending on the efficiency of the apparatus. The whisky or brandy addict used to daily doses of his 75 per cent proof spirit would, if he tried drinking home-distilled spirit, be knocked sideways by perhaps as little as one-eighth of what he is used to. *And the effect might be as disastrous as consuming methylated spirit or even petrol.* We have all read of people dying as a result of siphoning petrol from the tank of a car.

I am often asked what would be the result of distilling some of a wine in order to 'fortify' the rest. And my answer is always, 'Disappointing.' Not only is it a waste of good wine, but the act of making the wine stronger by adding spirit usually ruins the flavour. The alcohol breaks down various chemical matter important to the wine's flavour.

A friend of mine prides himself on the kick in his wines; kick there is, and precious little else. So don't be tempted to produce alcohol at the expense of flavour.

Wines made with the recipes in this book will be as strong as anybody would wish a wine to be.

The present laws relating to home wine-making let you make all the wine you want, free of tax and licence, but it must be consumed on the premises where it was made. It must not be sold. It cannot be given away – not so much as a bottle for raffling at a church bazaar.

That is the law – even if it isn't common sense. So if you take a bottle of parsnip wine round to a friend at Christmas, wrap it up well!

13
The Scientific Approach

I have often been accused of complicating simple matters. This is untrue, for wine-making is a very complicated business, yet simple enough when it is fully understood. Thousands of people believe that making wine is merely a matter of producing a liquid containing sugar, flavouring mediums and yeast and then allowing the wine to make itself under any sort of unhygienic conditions. Readers will know by now how false this belief really is, and they will not be surprised to learn that there is quite a lot of chemistry in the 'know-how' of wine-making.

The average home producer need not bother about much of this – indeed he will most likely make better wines for knowing nothing of it. But some familiarity with the chemical processes involved is necessary.

The partial sterilization of juices and the chemical preservation of wines which I am about to describe I use myself with complete safety and unfailing success. In using such methods we are merely copying those used by the trade.

STERILIZING THE JUICES

To destroy all the harmful bacteria in a fruit-juice-and-water mixture, it would have to be boiled for at least fifteen minutes, and the natural flavour of the juice would be ruined. The wine would have a 'cooked' flavour. The long periods of boiling when bottling fruits are intended to destroy bacteria which might begin to turn the bottled fruits into sour wine; the consequent stewed-fruit flavour is the natural and desired outcome.

Our aim then, as is the trade's, must be not so much the complete destruction of harmful bacteria, but the bringing about of conditions in which they cannot do their work, and in which the yeast can ferment the juice unmolested.

In Chapter 1 I advised boiling the juice for short periods, and this gives excellent safeguard. This, together with the use of sulphur dioxide for sterilizing bottles, etc., has always given me 100 per cent success.

But even boiling for very short periods sometimes has an adverse effect on certain fruit juices, and here is where sulphur dioxide comes in. As it is used for the home preserving of fruit it is quite safe to use in winemaking. Campden fruit-preserving tablets contain 50 per cent sulphur dioxide; two of these tablets, when crushed and dissolved in a cupful of juice, can be added to one gallon of fruit-and-water mixture to sterilize it and at the same time allow a suitable yeast to ferment the juice. I am fortunate in always having a vigorous dried yeast available and I find that this will ferment a 'must' containing the above amount of sulphur dioxide. Wine yeasts (of which I have something to say on page 97) are propagated under laboratory conditions and in the proximity of sulphur; these yeasts will then withstand this small dose of sulphur.

Readers unable to obtain a sulphur-dioxide solution from their chemists can easily make up a solution for themselves by dissolving an ounce of sodium metabisulphite (about 8d. from any chemist) in half a gallon of warm water. If you do this, try to use a glass-stoppered half-gallon bottle (about 1s. 6d.) and leave a couple of inches to spare at the top. This solution can be used and re-used for ages – until there is no whiff of the gas when smelled carefully. Never take a good sniff of this stuff as it can knock some people off their feet. I find that the odour is strongest when the bottles are rinsed out (see p. 12), so be careful. Where Campden tablets are recommended to be added to a must it is best to use them instead of some of the stock solution diluted, as these give greater accuracy.

Should you prefer to rid the juice of this sulphur and to ferment, say, with baker's yeast, you have merely to pour the 'must' from one vessel to another once or twice to liberate the gas. It should be borne in mind that harmful bacteria reaching the fermenting 'must' during later stages might not be prevented from doing damage if the sulphur has been removed. It is best to leave the sulphur dioxide where it is for the time being.

The advantage of using sulphur dioxide is that we are enabled to ferment the whole mixture, skins, pips and fleshy pith, with the result that we get much more flavour and more desirable chemical matter from our fruits. Besides all this, since we are not boiling our juices and therefore have no need to fear pectin, the tedium of straining through a jelly-bag is done away with.

Straining the fermenting 'must' after fourteen days' fermentation will liberate excess sulphur dioxide, leaving a pure, healthy, fermenting 'must'.

After straining, fermentation may slow down or stop for a little while, but it will soon get going again. The airing given during straining often gives rise to a very vigorous ferment, which, at this stage, is not to be encouraged.

Safety of the wine from now on is most important; the best plan is to put the strained fermenting wine into stone jars or large glass bottles which have been sterilized, and to fit fermentation locks. These will control fermentation and keep all harmful bacteria at bay. You may, if you wish, leave the strained wine for twenty-four hours to allow much waste matter to settle, and then siphon off the clearer wine into fresh jars before fitting the fermentation locks. If you do this, keep the wine well covered.

Fermentation Locks

The whole idea of using fermentation locks is to exclude all air and therefore all harmful bacteria from the wine: so we must ensure airtight sealing, and this is easily effected with a hot screw-driver and plenty of sealing-wax. Run sealing-wax round the point where the lock enters the bung and round the join where the bung enters the jar. After the lock is fitted, a little water is poured into it (see illustration on p. 95). As fermentation continues the excess carbon-dioxide gas forces its way through the water in the form of bubbles.

It is quite impossible to drill a cork or cork-bung with drills intended for wood or steel; special tools are needed. However, this difficulty may be overcome by burning a hole through the bung with a hot (not red-hot) iron about half the thickness of the glass stem. The resulting hole is then the right size. Start at the narrow end and try to keep straight. Since the wine is quite safe where it is, there is no need to hurry fermentation – in fact it is best to allow a rather cooler ferment, as a warm, and therefore vigorous, ferment often causes froth to be forced up into the fermentation lock.

When all fermentation has ceased, I find it best to soften the sealing-wax round the lock and to ease this out with a twisting movement. I then put a spigot in its place. This is pressed in firmly and sealed with sealing-wax. The wine is then put in a cool place to clear.

Beginners are always impatient to get their wines clear and into bottles; experienced wine-makers will know that it is best to leave the wine at least six months before bottling it – a year is even better.

Another advantage in using fermentation locks is that they not only keep all air and therefore all harmful bacteria from the wine, but they also prevent any bacteria that may be present in the 'must' at the time of fitting the lock from doing any damage. Bacteria cannot live without air, whereas yeast can both live and work without it.

Many people successfully make wine in this way without sulphiting the juices, but by preparing the 'must' and carrying on the whole of fermentation under fermentation locks. I do not recommend this method, for I have found that any wild yeast already present will do its damage nevertheless. In any case even if yeast can live and work without air, it does its work far better with plenty of air during the early stages – say for the first seven or fourteen days.

It is true that a great deal of air is put into the 'must' when the fruit is crushed, but this is probably used up too soon to be of much use.

I am in favour of sulphiting the juices and then carrying on the ferment in an 'open' tub, stirring it occasionally before fitting the locks. The value of the fermentation lock will never be disputed, but it should not be used as an alternative to taking reasonable precautions against spoilage.

Utensils

Earthenware vessels (crocks), china vessels and polythene pails are quite suitable for fermenting a 'must' containing sulphur dioxide. Wooden tubs may be used but these must be scrubbed well inside with pure (boiled) water before and after use, and exposed to sulphur fumes before a fresh brew is put into them. Specially prepared sulphur matches are obtainable, but if this job has to be carried out indoors you might find the fumes more than you can put up with.

Wooden vessels must not be rinsed in a solution of sulphur dioxide because it will soak into the wood and may destroy the yeast in the 'must'. It will probably flavour the wine too. You must remember that metals *must not come into contact with a brew containing sulphur dioxide.* Stir with a wooden or polythene spoon.

When you put the clear wine into bottles which have been sterilized with sulphur dioxide and then rinsed with boiled water, a tiny amount of SO_2 will be left in the air-space between the wine and the cork; cork each bottle immediately to capture and retain this gas for its protective properties. Airtight sealing of bottles as described in Chapter 1 is still essential.

Preserving Wines With SO_2

I have found that by boiling juices, sterilizing bottles, jars and corks, and ensuring airtight sealing of the bottled wine – as in Chapter 1 – and by using the methods described here, my wines are rendered immune from attacks by harmful bacteria however long I may choose to keep them.

Nevertheless, a word about preserving wines with sulphur dioxide must be included. The limit of SO_2 allowed by law in alcoholic wines is four hundred and fifty parts per million (450 parts SO_2 to 1,000,000 parts wine). More than two hundred and fifty parts per million would probably spoil the flavour of the wine. Although I no longer preserve my wines, I have used two hundred parts per million without there being the slightest trace of it in the finished wine poured into a glass.

A friend of mine – new to wine-making – who refuses to use SO_2 in his 'must', tastes his wines almost every week and confesses that 'the slightest sharpness makes me nearly have kittens over acetic bacteria, and in go the Campden tablets'. I have not yet found the heart (or heartlessness) to tell him that once the change has begun there is no control. To get approximately 200 parts SO_2 to 1,000,000 in one gallon of wine using Campden

a. Cork with the hole drilled through it.

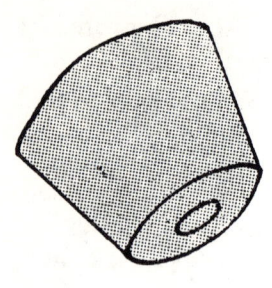

b. Cork fitted to the lock. Note that the long end of the lock is pushed through the cork.

1. *Fitting the fermentation lock.*

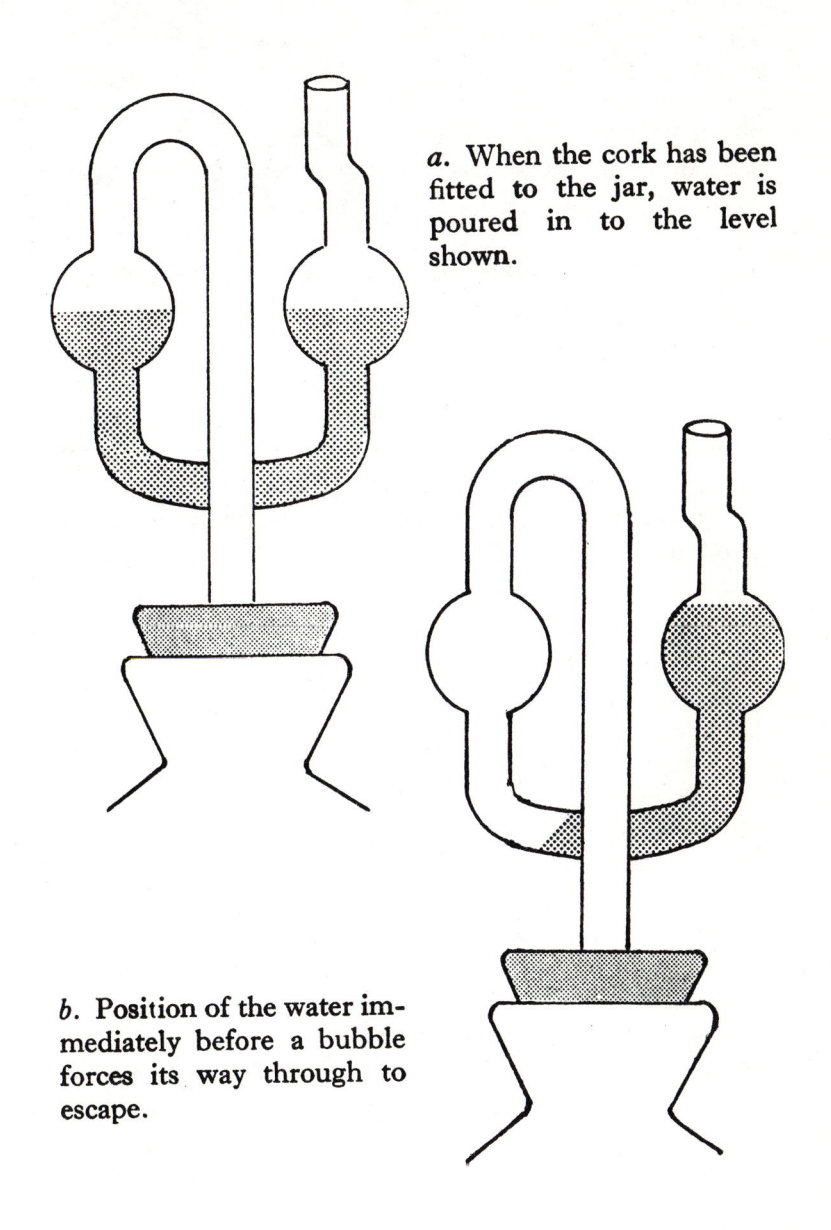

a. When the cork has been fitted to the jar, water is poured in to the level shown.

b. Position of the water immediately before a bubble forces its way through to escape.

2. *The fitted lock.*

fruit-preserving tablets, crush three and a half tablets and dissolve the powder in a little of the wine, and then pour this into the rest of the wine as soon as fermentation has ceased. Whether this amount will affect the taste depends on the strength of flavour of the wine so treated.

Root Wines and the Scientific Approach

All the root-wine recipes call for boiling of the ingredients. Therefore there is no need for sulphur dioxide in the fermenting liquid – I can hardly call it 'must' – provided the brew is kept well covered. With these recipes we merely fit fermentation locks after we have put the strained wine into stone jars at the end of the fourteen days' fermentation period. However, if you insist on using it, SO_2 can be added when the brew has cooled and before the yeast is added.

Fruit Wines and the Scientific Approach

The procedure when making fruit wines is as follows. Select the fruit, crush it, and add the dissolved Campden tablets. Leave as it is or liberate the gas by pouring from one vessel to another once or twice. Boil the water, or heat it sufficiently to dissolve the sugar quickly. Put in the sugar and when this is dissolved and the liquid is quite cool, add the crushed fruit. Add the yeast and ferment for fourteen days. Then strain it, put the strained wine into stone jars or large glass bottles and fit fermentation locks.

Allow the fermentation to complete itself. Remove the lock, plug the hole with a spigot, and seal with sealing wax.

Leave in a cool place for six months or a year and then bottle.

Note: the sulphiting method often proves unsatisfactory when used to make *flower wines*. Always follow the directions given in Chapter 1 when making these.

Readers not wishing to use sulphur dioxide in the fermenting 'must', may use the method of producing the wines detailed in Chapter 1 and fit fermentation locks when the still fermenting wine is put into stone jars.

As will be seen, there are many methods and each has its own advantage. Once the fundamental principles of wine-making are fully understood the operator will please himself how he makes his wine, but bearing in mind the need for sterility throughout the process.

Wine Yeasts

Baker's yeast is most frequently used by the average home wine-maker, chiefly because he is unaware that there are yeasts especially prepared for his purpose.

There are several varieties of wine yeast, and while these are intended expressly for the makers of grape wines, they may be used with considerable advantage when making wines from other fruits. I have used baker's yeast, brewer's barm and wine yeasts for root wines, flower wines, dried-fruit wines and for wines made with a mixture of roots, dried fruit and fresh fruits (as in the Jungle Juice recipes), and all with much the same results. But there was marked improvement in flavour and bouquet when the hedgerow fruits were fermented with wine yeasts.

Readers new to wine yeast would do well to try an all-purpose wine yeast suitable for making red or white wines and then, as experience allows, specialize with selected fruit and a special yeast culture. Only after experiment in this field will it be possible to decide which yeasts are needed to ferment to the best advantage the fruits of one's choice.

Special cultures are usually supplied in tubes or bottles and may be used for one to twenty gallons. By following the directions provided by the supplier, these yeasts may be used and re-used, and the small initial cash outlay will be well worth while. Dried wine yeasts in tablet form would be ideal for the beginner's use.

It is impossible to decide in advance which yeast to choose, for much depends on the result you want to obtain. Naturally, the reader will choose a port yeast for fermenting a fruit which would in the normal way produce a port-style wine – plums, damsons, elderberries, etc. Amongst the various wine yeasts available are:

>Sherry yeast
>Champagne yeast
>Madeira yeast

Wine yeasts are usually more tolerant to alcohol than baker's yeast and may allow for as much as 18 per cent alcohol, or even a little more.

People who are used to making wines with baker's yeast are familiar with the customary vigorous ferment, with its savage hissing and, sometimes, masses of froth. They should not expect the same from a wine yeast; these seldom make much of a show, but get on with the job quietly and effectively, taking perhaps rather a long time over it. If fermentation locks are used there is no hurry, because the wines will be perfectly safe under them.

In subsequent chapters I recommend using various dried wine yeasts or an all-purpose wine yeast – 'started' as described below – and I also advise the use of yeast nutrient (see p. 100). But these are only recommendations, and you may not wish or be able to follow them exactly.

So you can omit the nutrient if you wish; and if you would rather not stock up with a variety of wine yeasts you can use an all-purpose one instead. Or you may use a wine yeast of your own choosing where I have selected an all-purpose yeast or the one I, personally, consider most suitable. In other words, you can move about **a bit of your own accord without fear of failure.**

My recommendations are for what I consider the *best* results – and certainly I am rarely disappointed in my wine – but average results are readily obtained when the above variations are employed.

Personal taste is the main factor and in this the reader has only himself to please. He is lucky: I have to satisfy the exacting palate of many friends, relatives and acquaintances, besides that of a most discerning wife, who keeps me on my toes.

Yeast Starter

It is best to prepare the yeast three or four days ahead of actually adding it to the must. The idea here is to get what we call a nucleus fermentation on the go ready to take possession of the must at the very beginning. A previously prepared yeast is already working at the time it is put into the must; and within an hour or so the whole lot is in a state of active fermentation. If the yeast tablet is merely crushed and added dry, the start of the vigorous ferment might be delayed several days.

For practical purposes the method is the same when dried wine yeasts are used or when one of the more expensive bottle culture wine yeasts is used. Some suppliers favour a slightly different method of starting their yeasts, and if they do, they will provide the fullest directions with their products, so you need not worry. In any case, it will not vary much from the directions which follow.

Take a clean, freshly sterilized bottle, about a quarter-pint size, and three-parts fill this with boiled water in which has been dissolved a dessertspoonful of sugar. Then add the yeast tablet. Plug the neck of the bottle with cotton wool – this is most important; remember that wild yeast and bacteria can reach this ferment if it is not protected.

After a while the water will become cloudy; evidence that the yeast is becoming active. Shake the bottle gently once or twice a day.

Yeast Nutrient

When wines are fermenting under locks the yeast is deprived of air, and may need a little stimulant to help it along. In any case, fruit juices and 'must' – mixtures of fruit and water – other than that produced by crushing grapes lack to some extent the desirable chemical matter and other substances important to the satisfactory growth of the yeast. This deficiency may be made up by the introduction of a yeast nutrient. Many experienced wine-makers are satisfied to add a little citric acid or tartaric acid, but there is something to be said for using a proper nutrient, especially when baker's yeast is being used.

A nutrient used with wine yeasts to ferment various wild and cultivated fruits (other than grapes) produces finer wines than those fermented with wine yeasts alone. And experiments prove that a nutrient used with baker's yeast produces far better wines than when baker's yeast alone is used. I am giving here the formula of the nutrient I use for one or two gallons of wine:

Tartaric acid	40 grains
Ammonium sulphate	30 grains
Magnesium sulphate	4 grains
Citric acid	27 grains
Potassium phosphate	15 grains

Any chemist will make it up for you.

The nutrient may be added at the same time as the yeast or it may be added at the time the fermenting wine is put under fermentation locks.

Yeast nutrient tablets – which might prove cheaper – may be obtained in phials of eight for about 1s. 6d., usually enough for ten gallons of wine; one for one gallon and so on, four for five gallons and eight for ten.

Water

An adjustment to certain recipes will be necessary if you decide to sulphur the juices as I advise in this chapter. Since we are not boiling our fruit-and-water mixtures there will be no evaporation, and since we shall be using fermentation locks after a while, there will be less evaporation than there would be if we were carrying out the entire fermentation without them. So we shall not require that extra quart or pint. The amount of fruit recommended in the recipes remains the same, but in all cases one gallon of water only will be needed, or even less.

Filtering

There are various filtering media on the market – papers, asbestos pulps, pads, etc. – and one often reads of the need to filter finished wines. I do not agree with this, because the flavour is usually impaired; also, the wine can absorb too much air during the time needed for filtering. In any case, filtering exposes wines to undesirable yeast and bacteria, and a finished wine should not need filtering.

However, it is a good thing to filter juices before making them into wines, since this means that every particle of pectin-bearing fruit is removed. As I explained in Chapter 1, fruit contains pectin; so that if particles of fruit remain in the juice when it is boiled there is the risk that pectin will be boiled into the juice, and the wine made from it will not clear.

I have recommended jelly-bag straining in the recipes, and this is usually sufficient, but filtering is just as good if you prefer it.

Three Scientific Methods

It will be noted that, in the following methods, all the sugar is not added at once; this is because wine yeasts do not like a lot of sugar to work on all at once. Too much sugar at the outset might retard fermentation or even prevent it altogether. Or it might get going and then stop.

Method 1. The yeast starter is ready and you have decided which wine to make. You have the recipe handy.

Crush the fruits and add *half* the amount of water prescribed in the recipe. Mix well together and leave to stand for an hour. Then press through a coarse cloth. Wring this out as tightly as you can to get the maximum amount of juice.

Having squeezed out the juice, boil half the remaining water and dissolve half the amount of sugar to be used in this. This will be three-quarters of the water used so far, and half the sugar. Stir until the sugar is dissolved and add this sugar-water (syrup) to the strained juice.

Crush one Campden tablet with a wooden spoon or the bone handle of a knife and dissolve this in a few drops of water. Then stir this into the liquid.

If the must – as it has now become – is cool, add the yeast starter and nutrient tablet. Cover the fermenting vessel with a double thickness of blanketing and tie this down securely and tightly. If a heavy board is available rest this on top of the vessel. Put the must in a warm place and leave undisturbed for seven days.

Now boil the other half of the sugar in the remaining quarter of the water. When all is dissolved allow to cool and then pour this into the fermenting must.

Cover again as before and leave for twelve or twenty-four hours, whichever suits you best. Then put the wine into a stone or glass jar or bottles. In the ordinary way, this is the time to fit the fermentation lock; and I do strongly recommend readers to do this. But if the lock is not used, cover the tops of the jars with a piece of cloth measuring about three inches each way. On top of this put a knob of cotton wool; press this flat so that it overlaps the rim of the jar and then place another piece of cloth over this and press down all round. Tie tightly with thin string. If you wind the string round the necks of the bottles several times, so much the better.

Put the jars or bottles in a warm place and leave until all fermentation has ceased.

If large glass bottles (carboys) are used, fermentation may be watched with interest and the beginner will be able to tell when fermentation has ceased, i.e. when no more tiny bubbles are rising to the surface. When this happens, the covers must be removed, the bung is pressed home as hard as can be and the bottle or jar is sealed with sealing or candle wax. The wine is then put into the coolest spot in the house for three months. By this time it will be clear and ready for bottling.

Method 2. When this method is used, the whole of the crushed fruit is fermented and this is carried on in a fermenting vessel for the first few days.

Crush the fruit and set aside in the fermenting vessel. Now boil three-quarters of the water and dissolve in this half the amount of sugar prescribed in the recipe. Allow it to cool and pour into the fruit.

Crush one Campden tablet with a wooden spoon or the bone handle of a knife; dissolve this in a little water and pour into the must. Then add the yeast starter and nutrient tablet. Cover this as directed in Method 1 and leave to ferment for four to seven days according to the recipe.

Then strain the fermenting must through a coarse cloth and wring every drop of juice out of it. Pour this into a stone jar or carboy.

Now boil the other quarter of the water and dissolve the other half of the sugar in this. Make sure all the sugar is dissolved and allow this sugar-water (syrup) to cool. Then pour it into the rest.

When this has been done fit the fermentation lock or cover as directed in Method 1.

The wine must then be returned to its warm place to finish fermenting. This should be all over in three months, but it might take a good deal longer. When fermentation has ceased, you should remove the lock by warming the wax and easing the lock out in a twisting movement, or you can remove bung and lock completely and hammer in a new bung. If only the lock is removed the hole must be filled with a spigot, or spile as it is sometimes called. Either way, the new bung or spile must be sealed in with sealing wax or candle wax.

If you wish, you may transfer the wine to a new carboy as soon as fermentation has ceased. If the wine is reasonably clear it may be left for six months before bottling.

Method 3. Crush the fruits and strain out every drop of juice. Then boil three-quarters of the water and dissolve half the sugar in it. Allow to cool, then pour this syrup into the strained juice.

Add the yeast starter and nutrient tablet. Pour the lot into a stone jar or carboy and fit the fermentation lock. Put in a warm place and ferment for seven days. Then boil the other quarter of the water and dissolve in this the other half of the sugar. Make sure all the sugar is dissolved. Allow this syrup to cool and pour it into the bulk of the liquid.

Refit the fermentation lock, return the jar to its warm place and allow fermentation to continue until it is finished. Then transfer to another jar and store in a cool place for three months before bottling.

Campden tablets are not needed when using this method.

It will be clear to the reader that he can borrow half of one method and tack it on to the next and make his wine in practically any way he wishes. There is nothing like personal experience and experiment with different methods to enable him to decide which one he likes best or which is most convenient to himself.

In the recipes I shall cover certain points again so that the reader will not be left in doubt.

For Your Own Recipes

14
Fruit Wines the Modern Way

As will be seen, any of the three methods described in Chapter 13 may be used with these recipes, but it must be borne in mind that to produce a port or burgundy the skins of the fruit must be fermented for a time (Method 2); and that some fruits are more suitable for making these wine types than are others (see p. 184).

BLACKBERRY PORT

4 or 5 lb. blackberries · 7 pints water
4 lb. sugar · port yeast · nutrient
Campden tablet

Use *Method* 2. Ferment on the skins for seven days, then crush, wring out dry and add the rest of the sugar and water in the form of syrup to the strained juice. Transfer to a jar and fit the fermentation lock or cover as directed and leave until all fermentation has ceased.

BLACKBERRY PORT

3 lb. blackberries · 2 lb. elderberries
7 pints water · port yeast · nutrient
Campden tablet

Use *Method* 2. Ferment on the skins for ten days. Then wring out dry, make a syrup of the rest of the sugar and water and add this to the strained juice. Transfer to a jar and fit the fermentation lock or cover as directed and leave until all fermentation has ceased.

Blackberry Burgundy

4 lb. blackberries • 3½ lb. sugar
7 pints water • burgundy yeast • nutrient
Campden tablet

Use *Method* 2. Ferment on the skins for five days. Then strain, wring out dry and add the rest of the sugar and water as syrup to the strained juice. Then proceed as for *Blackberry Port* above.

Spiced Blackberry Wine

For a spiced blackberry wine you must decide for yourself the flavouring you prefer and the strength of such flavouring. It is best not to exceed the amount suggested otherwise you might find the wine rather too strongly flavoured. If the flavour is not quite strong enough you can use more next time.

3½ lb. blackberries • 3½ lb. sugar • 7 pints water
1 clove, or 1–3 drops of ginger essence
juice of 2 lemons • all-purpose wine yeast
nutrient • Campden tablet

Use *Method* 2. Ferment on the skins for four days. When the must has been strained and the pulp wrung out dry, add the strained juice of the lemons and the clove or ginger. Then transfer to a jar. Add the rest of the water and sugar as syrup. Fit fermentation lock or cover as directed and leave until all fermentation has ceased.

Blackberry Sweet Dessert

3 lb. blackberries • 4 lb. sugar • 7 pints water
malaga yeast • nutrient • Campden tablet

Use *Method* 1. Ferment the diluted juice for seven days, then add the rest of the sugar and water and transfer to a jar. Fit the fermentation lock or cover as directed and leave until all fermentation has ceased.

Blackberry Dry Table Wine

3 lb. blackberries · 1 gallon water · 3 lb. sugar
sherry yeast · nutrient · Campden tablet

Use *Method* 1. Ferment the diluted juice for fourteen days, then make syrup of the rest of the sugar and water and add this to the rest. Put into a jar and fit the fermentation lock or cover as directed and leave until all fermentation has ceased.

Cherry, Sweet Dessert

This recipe makes a most attractive sweet wine.

10 lb. black cherries · 7 pints water · 4 lb. sugar
bordeaux yeast · nutrient · Campden tablet

This wine is often improved by adding a quarter ounce of citric acid, but this is a matter of choice.

Use *Method* 1. Ferment the diluted juice for seven days before transferring to a jar. Then add the rest of the sugar and water as syrup. If citric acid is used, add this before adding the yeast starter.

When the syrup (sugar and water) has been added fit the fermentation lock or cover as directed and leave until all fermentation has ceased.

Cherry Wine, Dry

8 lb. black cherries · 7 pints water · 3 lb. sugar
sherry yeast · nutrient · Campden tablet

Use *Method* 1. Ferment the diluted juice for ten days. Then make a syrup of the rest of the sugar and water and add this to the rest. Transfer to a jar, fit the fermentation lock or cover as directed and leave until all fermentation has ceased.

Blackcurrant Port

6 lb. blackcurrants • 4½ lb. sugar • 7 pints water
port yeast • nutrient • Campden tablet

Use *Method 2*. Ferment the crushed pulp for seven days, then strain, wring out dry and add the rest of the sugar and water to the juice in the form of syrup. Fit the fermentation lock or cover as directed and leave to finish fermenting.

Blackcurrant Port

3½ lb. blackcurrants • 1½ lb. raisins • 3 lb. sugar
1 gallon water • port yeast • nutrient
Campden tablet

Use *Method 2*. Ferment the crushed blackcurrants for ten days. Then strain and wring out dry. Transfer the strained wine to a jar and add the rest of the sugar and water in the form of syrup. Fit the fermentation lock or cover as directed and leave until all fermentation has ceased.

Blackcurrant, Sweet Dessert

3½ lb. blackcurrants • 3 lb. grapes (any sort)
7 pints water • 3½ lb. sugar • malaga or port yeast
nutrient • Campden tablet

Use *Method 1*. Crush both fruits and mix well together, then ferment the strained and diluted juice for ten days. Make a syrup of the rest of the sugar and water and add this to the bulk. Transfer to a jar and fit the fermentation lock or cover as directed and leave until all fermentation has ceased.

Blackcurrant Dry Table Wine

3½ lb. blackcurrants • 3 lb. sugar
7 pints water • sherry yeast • nutrient
Campden tablet

Use *Method* 1. Ferment the strained and diluted juice for seven days. Make a syrup of the rest of the sugar and water and add this to the rest. Then transfer to a jar and fit the fermentation lock or cover as directed and leave until all fermentation has ceased.

Redcurrant Light Dessert Wine

3½ lb. redcurrants • 7 pints water • 3½ lb. sugar
madeira or malaga yeast • nutrient
Campden tablet

Use *Method* 1. Ferment the strained and diluted juice for fourteen days. Then make a syrup of the rest of the sugar and water and add this. Transfer to a jar and fit the fermentation lock or cover as directed and leave until all fermentation has ceased.

Redcurrant Table Wine

4 lb. redcurrants • 4 lb. sugar • 1 gallon water
burgundy yeast • nutrient • Campden tablet

Use *Method* 1. Ferment the diluted juice for seven days and then transfer to a jar. Add the rest of the water and sugar in the form of syrup. Fit fermentation lock or cover as directed and leave until all fermentation has ceased.

Redcurrant Sweet Dessert Wine

3½ lb. redcurrants • 4 lb. sugar • 7 pints water
malaga yeast • nutrient • Campden tablet

Use *Method* 1. Ferment the diluted juice for seven days and then transfer to a jar. Add the rest of the sugar and water in the form of syrup, fit the fermentation lock or cover as directed and leave until all fermentation has ceased.

Whitecurrant Light Dessert Wine

5 lb. whitecurrants · 3½ lb. sugar
7 pints water · sherry yeast · nutrient
Campden tablet

Use *Method* 1. Ferment the diluted juice for seven days and then transfer to a jar. Add the rest of the water and sugar in the form of a syrup. Then fit the fermentation lock or cover as directed and leave until all fermentation has ceased.

Whitecurrant Sweet Dessert Wine

6 lb. whitecurrants · 4 lb. sugar · 7 pints water
malaga yeast · nutrient · Campden tablet

Use *Method* 1. Ferment the diluted juice for seven days and then transfer to a jar. Add the rest of the sugar and water in the form of a syrup. Then fit the fermentation lock or cover as directed and leave until all fermentation has ceased.

Whitecurrant Dry Table Wine

4 lb. whitecurrants · 3 lb. sugar · 7 pints water
sherry yeast · nutrient · Campden tablet

Use *Method* 1. Ferment the strained, diluted juice for ten days. Then add the rest of the sugar and water in the form of a syrup and transfer to a jar. Fit the fermentation lock or cover as directed and leave until all fermentation has ceased.

Damson Port

8 lb. damsons · 7 pints water · 4 lb. sugar
port yeast · nutrient · Campden tablet

Use *Method* 2. Ferment the crushed fruit for ten days. Then strain, wring out dry and add the rest of the sugar and water in the form of a syrup to the strained wine. Transfer to a jar, fit the fermentation lock or cover as directed and leave until all fermentation has ceased.

Damson Port

6 lb. damsons • 1 lb. raisins • 1 gallon water
4 lb. sugar • port yeast • nutrient
Campden tablet

Use *Method 2*. Ferment the crushed damsons together with the chopped raisins for fourteen days. Then strain, wring out dry and add the rest of the sugar and water in the form of a syrup. Transfer to a jar and fit the fermentation lock or cover as directed and leave until all fermentation has ceased.

Damson Dry Table Wine

This is a pleasing dry wine that should be made more than it is.

4 lb. damsons • 2½ lb. sugar • 7 pints water
sherry yeast • nutrient • Campden tablet

Use *Method 1*. Ferment the strained, diluted juice for ten days. Then make a syrup of the rest of the sugar and water and add this to the rest. Transfer to a jar and fit fermentation lock or cover as directed and leave until all fermentation has ceased.

Damson and Elderberry (or Grape) Port

4 lb. damsons • 1½ lb. elderberries (or 3 lb. black grapes)
7 pints water • 4 lb. sugar
port or burgundy yeast • nutrient
Campden tablet

Use *Method 2*. Crush the fruits, mix well together, and ferment the pulp for ten days. Then strain, wring out dry and transfer the wine to a jar. Add the rest of the sugar and water in the form of a syrup and fit the fermentation lock or cover as directed and then leave until all fermentation has ceased.

Damson and Dried Prune Burgundy

4 lb. damsons • 2 lb. dried prunes
1 gallon water • 3½ lb. sugar • burgundy yeast
nutrient • Campden tablet

Use *Method 2*. Crush the damsons, add the cut-up prunes and ferment the pulp for ten days. Then strain, wring out dry and transfer the wine to a jar. Add the rest of the sugar and water in the form of a syrup and fit the fermentation lock or cover as directed and leave until all fermentation has ceased.

Raspberry Table Wine

5 lb. raspberries • 7 pints water • 3½ lb. sugar
burgundy yeast • nutrient • Campden tablet

Use *Method 1*. Ferment the strained juice for fourteen days. Then make a syrup of the rest of the sugar and water and add this to the bulk. Transfer to a jar and fit the fermentation lock or cover as directed and leave until all fermentation has ceased.

Raspberry Sweet Dessert Wine

4 lb. raspberries • ½ lb. dates (or raisins)
3½ lb. sugar • 7 pints water • malaga yeast
nutrient • Campden tablet

Use *Method 1*. Ferment the strained, diluted raspberry juice for ten days. Then add the dates and leave to ferment a further ten days. Then strain, wring out dry and add the rest of the sugar and water in the form of a syrup. Transfer to a jar and fit the fermentation lock or cover as directed and leave until all fermentation has ceased.

Raspberry Dry Table Wine

3½ lb. raspberries · 3 lb. sugar · 7 pints water
sherry yeast · nutrient · Campden tablet

Use *Method* 1. Ferment the diluted juice for ten days. Then make a syrup of the rest of the water and sugar and add this to the rest. Pour into a jar and fit the fermentation lock or cover as directed and leave until all fermentation has ceased.

Strawberry Wine

8 lb. strawberries · 7 pints water · 2½ lb. sugar
malaga yeast · nutrient · Campden tablet

Use *Method* 2. Ferment the pulp for ten days. Strain, wring out dry and add the rest of the sugar and water in the form of a syrup. Transfer to a jar and fit fermentation lock or cover as directed and leave until all fermentation has ceased.

Note. Strawberry wine is often improved by adding the juice of two lemons at the beginning.

Strawberry Wine (Dry)

6 lb. strawberries · 2 lemons · 7 pints water
2 lb. sugar · sherry yeast · nutrient
Campden tablet

Use *Method* 1. Ferment the strained, diluted juice together with the juice of the lemons for seven days.

Then make a syrup of the rest of the sugar and water and add this to the strained wine. Transfer to a jar and fit the fermentation lock or cover as directed and leave until all fermentation has ceased.

ELDERBERRY WINES

Elderberries make one of the oldest of known country wines – and surely one of the best, if not the very best of all. There are countless recipes and many methods of making the various wine types, using the one fruit only or mixing with other fruits. Elderberries are often made into spiced wines with cloves or ginger.

Among the following the reader will find an elderberry recipe to satisfy his discerning palate, and I do hope it is one of the first three, for I am especially fond of the wines I turn out each year from these recipes.

Readers with a little experience are urged to try out their own ideas, using elderberries as a base-fruit, and with raisins, prunes or dates or fresh fruit such as blackberries, damsons and grapes. If the reader will turn to page 113 he can use the DAMSON AND ELDERBERRY (OR GRAPE) PORT recipe as an example.

ELDERBERRY PORT

5 lb. elderberries • 7 pints water • $4\frac{1}{4}$ lb. sugar
port yeast • nutrient • Campden tablet

Use *Method* 2. Ferment the pulp for three days; then strain and wring out dry and continue to ferment in a tub for a further seven days. Then transfer to a jar and add the rest of the sugar and water in the form of syrup. Fit the fermentation lock or cover as directed and leave until all fermentation has ceased.

ELDERBERRY PORT

4 lb. elderberries • 1 gallon water • $4\frac{1}{2}$ lb. sugar
port yeast • nutrient • Campden tablet

Use *Method* 2. Ferment the pulp for ten days, then strain and wring out dry and add the rest of the water and sugar in the form of a syrup to the strained wine. Put into a jar and fit fermentation lock or cover as directed and leave until all fermentation has ceased.

Elderberry Sweet Dessert

3 lb. elderberries • 4½ lb. sugar • 1 gallon water
port or malaga yeast • Campden tablet

Use *Method* 1. Ferment the strained, diluted juice for fourteen days. Then make a syrup of the rest of the sugar and water and add this to the wine. Put into a jar and fit the fermentation lock or cover as directed and leave until all fermentation has ceased.

Elderberry Table Wine

3½ lb. elderberries • 3½ lb. sugar • 7 pints water
burgundy or tokay yeast • nutrient
Campden tablet

Use *Method* 1. Ferment the strained, diluted juice for ten days. Then make a syrup of the rest of the sugar and water and add this to the rest. Pour into a jar and fit the fermentation lock or cover as directed and leave until all fermentation has ceased.

Elderberry Dry Table Wine

3 lb. elderberries • 3 lb. sugar • 7 pints water
sherry yeast • nutrient • Campden tablet

Use *Method* 1. Ferment the strained, diluted juice for seven days. Then make a syrup of the rest of the water and sugar and add this to the rest. Pour into a jar and fit fermentation lock or cover as directed and leave until all fermentation has ceased.

Elderberry Wine

Light and very dry.

2½ lb. elderberries • 2 lb. sugar • 7 pints water
sherry yeast • nutrient • Campden tablet

Use *Method* 1. Ferment the strained, diluted juice for fourteen days. Then make a syrup of the rest of the sugar and water and add this to the rest. Transfer to a jar and fit fermentation lock or cover as directed and leave until all fermentation has ceased.

Note. If this turns out just a little too dry it may be sweetened with ordinary white sugar.

Warm a little of the wine and dissolve sugar in this; then add so much to each bottle, or the whole lot to the bulk. White sugar will not cloud the wine.

Apple Wine

10 lb. apples • 3½ lb. sugar • 7 pints water
1 clove • port yeast • nutrient
Campden tablet

Although a port yeast is used for this wine it will not, of course, resemble port.

A fairly sweet variety of apple is best for this one, but half sweet and half otherwise, mixed, will make a very nice wine. If only a not very sweet variety is available, use an extra ½ lb. of sugar.

Use *Method* 2. Core the apples (for we do not want to crush the pips). Chop and then crush them or put them through the mincer. Ferment the pulp for seven days, then strain and wring out dry and transfer the fermenting juice to a jar. Add the rest of the sugar and water in the form of a syrup.

Fit the fermentation lock or cover as directed and leave until all fermentation has ceased.

Pear Wine

10 lb. pears · juice of 2 lemons
7 pints water · 3½ lb. sugar · port yeast
nutrient · Campden tablet

Use *Method 2*. Add the lemon juice at the beginning and proceed as for Apple Wine above.

Plum Burgundy

7 lb. plums (any red variety will do –
weighed with the stones)
7 pints water · 4 lb. sugar · burgundy yeast
nutrient · Campden tablet

Use *Method 2*. Ferment the pulp for seven days, then strain and wring out dry and transfer the fermenting juice to a jar. Add the rest of the sugar and water in the form of syrup. Fit the fermentation lock or cover as directed and leave until all fermentation has ceased.

Rhubarb Table Wine

6 lb. rhubarb · 7 pints water · 4½ lb. sugar
sherry yeast · nutrient · Campden tablet

Use *Method 1*. Crush the rhubarb and allow it to soak for seven days in half the water, in which one Campden tablet has been dissolved. Then strain, wring out dry and warm the juice just enough to dissolve the first half of the sugar. Ferment this for fourteen days. Make syrup of the rest of the water and sugar and add this to the rest. Put into a jar and fit the fermentation lock or cover as directed and leave until all fermentation has ceased.

Rhubarb Wine

5 lb. rhubarb · 1 lb. raisins · 7 pints water
4 lb. sugar · sherry yeast · nutrient
Campden tablet

Use *Method 2*. Crush the rhubarb, chop the raisins and ferment the pulp for ten days. Strain, wring out dry and transfer to a jar. Add the rest of the sugar and water in the form of a syrup, then fit the fermentation lock or cover as directed and leave until all fermentation has ceased.

Plum Port

8 lb. plums (any variety, weighed with the stones)
3 lb. sugar • 7 pints water • port yeast
nutrient • Campden tablet

Use *Method 2*. Ferment the pulp for ten days, then strain, wring out dry and put the fermenting juice in a jar. Make syrup of the rest of the sugar and water and add this to the bulk. Fit the fermentation lock or cover as directed and leave until all fermentation has ceased.

Plum Port

6 lb. plums • 1 lb. raisins • 1 lb. prunes
3 lb. sugar • 1 gallon water • port yeast
nutrient • Campden tablet

Use *Method 2*. Crush the plums, cut up the prunes and chop the raisins. Then ferment the pulp for ten days. After this, strain, wring out dry and put the strained wine into a jar. Make a syrup of the rest of the water and sugar and add this to the rest. Fit the fermentation lock or cover as directed and leave until all fermentation has ceased.

Loganberry Burgundy

7 pints loganberries • 7 pints water
3½ lb. sugar • burgundy yeast • nutrient
Campden tablet

Use *Method 2*. Ferment the crushed pulp for ten days. Then strain, wring out dry and transfer the liquid to a jar. Add the rest of the sugar and water in the form of syrup. Fit fermentation lock or cover as directed and leave until all fermentation has ceased.

Loganberry Sweet Dessert Wine

6 pints loganberries · 7 pints water · 4 lb. sugar
malaga yeast · nutrient · Campden tablet

Use *Method* 1. Ferment the strained, diluted juice for fourteen days. Then make a syrup of the rest of the water and sugar and add it. Fit the fermentation lock or cover and then leave until all fermentation has ceased.

Loganberry Burgundy-Port

A very special burgundy-port-style wine may be made if you can spare a great many loganberries. Twelve pints are needed, and if you have this many I do hope you will try this recipe.

12 pints loganberries · 7 pints water
$3\frac{1}{2}$ lb. sugar · port or burgundy yeast
nutrient · Campden tablet

Use *Method* 2. Ferment the crushed pulp for ten days. Then strain, wring out dry and put into a jar. Make syrup of the remainder of the sugar and water and add this to the rest. Fit fermentation lock or cover as directed and leave until all fermentation has ceased.

Gooseberry Table Wine

8 lb. gooseberries · 7 pints water · $4\frac{1}{2}$ lb. sugar
tokay yeast · nutrient · Campden tablet

Use *Method* 1. Ferment the strained, diluted juice for seven days. Then make a syrup of the rest of the sugar and water and add this to the bulk. Transfer to a jar and fit the fermentation lock or cover as directed and leave until all fermentation has ceased.

Gooseberry Dessert Wine

4 lb. gooseberries · 1 lb. packet dates
4 lb. sugar · 7 pints water · sherry yeast
nutrient · Campden tablet

Use *Method* 2. Ferment the crushed gooseberries and chopped date blocks together for fourteen days. Then strain, wring out dry and put the wine into a jar. Make a syrup of the rest of sugar and water and add this to the rest. Fit the fermentation lock or cover as directed and leave until all fermentation has ceased.

Gooseberry Sherry

Well-ripened gooseberries are needed for this wine; those that have turned yellow – or red, according to variety. They should be fairly soft, but *not damaged*. Any damaged ones should be discarded, as these might well have mould forming in the damaged parts and this can cause trouble.

For a medium sweet to dry sherry type use three pounds of sugar; for a dry sherry use only two pounds.

6 lb. gooseberries · 7 pints water
2–3 lb. sugar as required · sherry yeast
nutrient · Campden tablet

Use *Method* 2. Ferment the pulp for ten days. Then strain and wring out dry and transfer to a jar. Add the rest of the sugar and water in the form of a syrup. Fit fermentation lock or cover as directed and leave until all fermentation has ceased.

WHORTLEBERRY WINES

Wines made with whortleberries (also known as 'hurts' or bilberries – and, I believe, as blaeberry or blueberry in Scotland) are every bit as good as those made with elderberries. Unfortunately, whereas the elderberry will grow in town gardens – in fact, almost anywhere – whortleberries will not. Let's hope that some enterprising nurseryman will carry out trials and finally produce a variety of whortleberry to grow as a cultivated fruit. This has been done with practically every other variety of fruit which was at one time wild.

For the benefit of those within easy reach of the wild whortleberries (I myself live within walking distance of the famous beauty spots of Leith Hill and Ewhurst where these purple-black berries abound) I am including the following recipes.

Whortleberry Burgundy

5 pints whortleberries • 7 pints water
3½ lb. sugar • burgundy yeast • nutrient
Campden tablet

Use *Method 2*. Ferment the pulp for seven days. Then strain, wring out dry and transfer the wine to a jar. Make a syrup of the remaining sugar and water and add this to the rest. Fit the fermentation lock or cover as directed and leave until all fermentation has ceased.

Whortleberry Port

7 pints whortleberries • 7 pints water
4 lb. sugar • ½ lb. packet dates
port yeast • nutrient • Campden tablet

Use *Method 2*. Ferment the crushed pulp, together with the chopped date block, for ten days. Then strain, wring out dry and put the wine into a jar. Make a syrup of the rest of the sugar and water and add this to the bulk. Fit fermentation lock or cover as directed and leave until all fermentation has ceased.

Whortleberry Light Table Wine

3 pints whortleberries • 3½ lb. sugar
7 pints water • malaga yeast • nutrient
Campden tablet

Use *Method* 1. Ferment the strained, diluted juice for ten days. Then make a syrup of the rest of the sugar and water and add this to the bulk. Put into a jar and fit fermentation lock or cover as directed and leave until all fermentation has ceased.

Whortleberry Sweet Dessert Wine

4 pints whortleberries • 4 lb. sugar
7 pints water • madeira or malaga yeast
nutrient • Campden tablet

Use *Method* 1. Ferment the strained, diluted juice for fourteen days. Make a syrup of the remaining water and sugar and add this to the rest. Put into a jar and fit the fermentation lock or cover as directed and leave until all fermentation has ceased.

For Your Own Recipes

For Your Own Recipes

15

Grape Wines

Ordinarily, sixteen to twenty pounds of grapes are needed to make one gallon of wine, and water is not usually added. If it is, sugar will also have to be added. The whole bunches, complete with stalks, are fermented in the crushed state for a time; the juice is then wrung out (crushed if a press is available), and the juice then fermented to completion.

If, for the sake of economy, water has to be added, sugar must also be added because we shall have reduced the sugar content by diluting the must.

Sixteen or even twenty pounds of grapes do not guarantee one gallon of wine; if the summer has been dry there will be less juice and more sugar. If the summer has been a wet one, there will be more juice and less sugar. It is here that the hydrometer comes in handy (see p. 158).

Much can be done by adding a quart of water to the lump of crushed pulp (this point will be covered in the recipes); if this is done we shall have to add a pound of sugar, or perhaps a little more.

The yeast on your grapes might be quite suitable for turning them into good wines, but the risk that there might be undesirable strains present must not be overlooked. It is far better to partially sterilize the must with one Campden tablet per gallon – one should be enough – and then to introduce an already prepared yeast starter.

Since the colour comes from the skins the process for a red wine will be as follows. Put sixteen to twenty pounds of grapes into a suitable vessel and crush them well – make sure all the individual fruits are crushed. Now crush and dissolve one Campden tablet and stir this into the must. Then add the already prepared yeast starter. Port or burgundy yeast is recommended, but the experienced reader may use the yeast of his choice. Yeast nutrient is not needed.

Allow fermentation to go on for seven days. During this time keep the must covered as already directed and, about once a day, push the 'cap' of grape skins under the surface and cover again at once.

After seven days the must should be pressed, but it is unlikely that my readers will have such a thing as a wine press. Straining and wringing out the pulp will be more in their line, and for this a strong coarse cloth is best so that every drop of juice can be wrung out without risk of the cloth bursting.

When all the juice has been wrung out, the lump of grape skins may be mixed with a quart of water; this is mixed well together and then wrung out as dry as possible.

One pound of sugar is dissolved in this thinner grape juice and this is then added to the bulk. If fermentation stops at this stage, do not worry; it will soon get going again.

The whole is now put into a stone jar or carboy, the fermentation lock fitted – or the jar covered as already advised – and fermentation allowed to go on till it is finished.

If you wish, you may leave the strained juice in the tub for twenty-four hours before putting it into the jar. If you do this you must use a funnel and pour gently so as to leave the heavy deposit that may have formed at the bottom of the tub.

When fermentation has ceased the wine should be siphoned off the lees into another jar. If one gallon only was made there will be a little less now. The best plan would be to fill a half-gallon jar and to put the rest into bottles. The wine may not be clear at this stage, but this does not matter. Seal the bottles and jar and store them on their sides in the coolest spot you have in the house. At the end of three months the wine should be crystal clear, and may be siphoned off into new bottles.

Standing them upright will disturb the lees lying along the sides of the bottles, but if they are left standing upright overnight the lees will have settled so that the wine may be siphoned off into freshly sterilized bottles, sealed with freshly boiled corks and put away on their sides again, where they should remain for another six months. A tiny amount of deposit may form during this time; if this happens, rebottle before using.

The method just described, and the amount of grapes mentioned, will make a very excellent wine; but the identical process with the exact amount of fruit will not necessarily produce an identical wine the following year. It may not vary greatly from year to year; if it does, the wise vintner will blend a few bottles of one year's wine with a few bottles of another year to get the wine type he is especially keen on.

To make a *white wine* from black grapes the juice only is fermented. The procedure is the same as for red wine except that the water is mixed with the grape pulp; the sugar is then dissolved in the thinner grape juice squeezed out of this and is added to the bulk before the yeast itself is added. Nutrient is not needed here, but one Campden tablet should be dissolved and added before the yeast is put in.

Fermentation is allowed to go on for seven to ten days; at this stage the must is put into a jar. Since no solids are present, there will be no need for straining, but it is a good plan to transfer the wine to the jar carefully so that not too much heavy deposit enters. At this stage it is wise to add a large teaspoonful of freshly made, fairly strong tea to make up for the tannin that would have been put into the wine if the skins had been fermented. Lack of tannin often makes white wines rather slower than others to clear.

After this, continue as for red wines.

If an abundance of grapes is not available the reader will find the following recipes helpful besides being well worth following. Some of the water should be saved and the sugar dissolved in this and added at the time the wine is put into a jar.

Recipe For a Red Wine – 1

9 lb. black grapes • 2 lb. raisins • 3 pints water
1 lb. sugar • port or burgundy yeast
Campden tablet

Use *Method 2*. Ferment the crushed grapes together with the chopped raisins for seven days. Then strain and wring out dry and transfer to a jar. Add the rest of the sugar and water in the form of a syrup.

Recipe For a Red Wine – 2

8 lb. black grapes • 3–5 lb. dried prunes
4 pints water • 1 lb. sugar
port or burgundy yeast • Campden tablet

Use *Method 2* and follow directions for Recipe 1.

Recipe For a Red Wine – 3

8 lb. black grapes • 1½ lb. raisins • 1½ lb. prunes
1 lb. sugar • 3 pints water • port yeast
Campden tablet

Use *Method 2* and follow the directions given for Recipe 1.

Readers are urged to make up their own recipes using the above as a guide and substituting dates for raisins.

16

That Stewed-fruit Flavour

This chapter deals with a method of making fruit wine quite distinct from anything already described in this book: don't confuse the two methods or try to use half of one and half of another.

Most people like the characteristic flavour of raw fruit to remain in the finished wines and, personally, I like this in most wines; indeed, it would not seem like wine if I could not detect at once the fruit used in its making. (With root wines this does not apply: potato wine never tastes of potatoes.)

The raw-fruit flavour is not as strong, of course, as when a gooseberry or blackcurrant is picked direct from the bush and eaten: the flavour merely underlies other flavours present. Now, the methods already described in this book produce wines in which the flavour of the raw fruits can be detected. But a great number of people like their wines flavoured slightly of stewed fruit – especially wines made from fruits ordinarily eaten raw. This stewed-fruit flavour, like the raw-fruit flavour, merely underlies other flavours present, and one can quite understand their liking for it.

This chapter has been included especially for these people.

As has already been mentioned, boiling the fruit itself often produces wines that prove almost impossible to clarify. We must not boil the fruit – only the carefully strained juice. In using this method we shall be going back rather than advancing in wine-making, but do not let us go back so far as to resort to the use of bakers' yeast. True, this yeast does make quite a good wine, as every home wine-maker will gladly verify, but wine yeast prepared as already directed will make *far better* wines.

The following recipes are somewhat similar to those in Chapter 5, but whereas there I recommended one ounce of bakers' yeast per gallon, here I shall recommend a suitable wine yeast.

It will be seen that the directions call for the use of a fermentation lock, and I do hope my readers will use this. If for some special reason they cannot, or do not wish to use it, they must cover their brews as directed on page 103.

It will be seen that after a certain interval the wine is put into a stone jar or glass carboy, and this will be necessary if fermentation locks are being used. If jars are not available, a number of bottles may be used and these will have to be covered with cloth and cotton wool as directed on page 12.

Once the wine has been put into bottles (or a jar fitted with a fermentation lock) it must remain undisturbed until all fermentation has ceased.

In these recipes part of the water and sugar is saved for adding later on. This is because wine yeasts do not handle a great deal of sugar at once at all well.

If you are not using wine yeasts, you may use bakers' yeast by crumbling it over the surface at the time given in the recipes for adding the yeast starter. But *do* try to use wine yeasts.

Campden tablets are not needed in the recipes in this chapter, since the liquids are sterilized by boiling.

Elderberry Wine

Rich, port-style.

4 lb. elderberries · 4 lb. sugar · 1 gallon water
port yeast · nutrient

Crush the berries, pour six pints of water over them and leave to soak overnight. Strain and wring out dry and put the strained juice through a jelly-bag. Leave to drain overnight if necessary. Do not squeeze. Bring this juice to boiling-point and simmer for four minutes. Put half the sugar in the fermenting vessel and pour over the hot juice. Stir until all the sugar is dissolved. Allow the brew to cool and then add the yeast starter and nutrient tablet.

Cover as directed and ferment for fourteen days. Then make a syrup of the rest of the water and sugar and add this to the bulk. Transfer to a jar and fit the fermentation lock or cover as directed and leave until all fermentation has ceased.

Elderberry Wine

Burgundy type.

3 quarts elderberries • 4 lb. sugar
1 gallon water • burgundy yeast • nutrient

Crush the berries, pour half the water over them and leave to soak overnight. Strain, wring out dry and put the juice through a jelly-bag. Mix the pulp with two pints of water and then wring this out also and put this juice through a jelly-bag. Then add this juice to the rest. Bring slowly to boiling-point – taking off any scum that rises – and simmer for three or four minutes.

Pour into the fermenting vessel and add half the sugar, stirring until all is dissolved.

Allow the brew to cool and then add the yeast starter and nutrient. Cover as directed and ferment for ten days. Then make a syrup of the rest of the sugar and water and add this to the rest. Finally, transfer to a jar and fit the fermentation lock or cover as directed and leave until all fermentation has ceased.

Elderberry Table Wine

3 lb. elderberries · 1 gallon water · 3 lb. sugar
malaga yeast · nutrient

Crush the berries and pour six pints of water over them. Stir well and leave to soak for twelve hours.

Strain and wring out dry and put the strained juice through a jelly-bag. Bring this juice just to boiling-point and cut off the heat at once.

Put half the sugar into the fermenting vessel and pour the hot juice over it. Stir until all the sugar is dissolved. Allow to cool and add the yeast starter and nutrient. Cover as directed and leave to ferment for seven days. Then make a syrup of the rest of the sugar and water and stir this into the rest. Transfer to a jar and fit the fermentation lock or cover as directed. Leave until all fermentation has ceased.

Damson and Elderberry Port

3 lb. damsons · 2 lb. elderberries
1 gallon water · 4 lb. sugar · port yeast
nutrient

Crush both the fruits, mixing them together. Boil six pints of water and when it has cooled pour it over the pulp and leave to soak overnight.

Strain and wring out dry and put the strained juice through a jelly-bag. Bring this strained juice to boiling-point and simmer for four minutes. Pour into the fermenting vessel and add half the sugar, stirring until all the sugar is dissolved. Allow to cool and then add the yeast starter and nutrient. Cover as directed and leave to ferment for ten days. Then make a syrup of the rest of the water and sugar and add this to the bulk. Transfer the lot to a jar and fit the fermentation lock or cover as directed. Leave until all fermentation has ceased.

Prune and Elderberry Port

2½ lb. prunes • 2½ lb. elderberries
3 lb. sugar • 1 gallon water • port yeast
nutrient

Pour half a gallon of boiling water over the prunes and leave to soak overnight. At the same time pour two pints of cold water over the crushed elderberries and leave these to soak overnight as well. Then crush both mixtures well and put them together.

Strain, wring out dry and then put the strained juice through a jelly-bag. Bring this juice to boiling-point and simmer for five minutes. Put half the sugar in the fermenting vessel, pour the hot juice over it and stir until all the sugar is dissolved. Allow to cool and then add the yeast starter and nutrient. Cover as directed and leave to ferment for ten days.

Make syrup of the rest of the sugar and water and add this to the bulk. Then transfer to a jar and fit the fermentation lock or cover as directed. Leave until all fermentation has ceased.

Raisin and Elderberry Wine

1½ lb. raisins • 2½ lb. elderberries
3 lb. sugar • 1 gallon water • burgundy yeast
nutrient

Crush the elderberries and pour over them six pints of boiled water that has cooled a bit. Leave to soak overnight. Strain and wring out dry and put the juice through a jelly-bag. Bring the strained juice to boiling-point and simmer for two minutes. Put half the sugar into the fermenting vessel and pour the hot juice over it, stirring until all the sugar is dissolved. Then put in the cut-up raisins.

Allow the brew to cool and then add the yeast starter

and nutrient. Cover as directed and ferment for fourteen days. Strain and wring out dry.

Make a syrup of the rest of the sugar and water and add this to the bulk. Pour into a jar and fit the fermentation lock or cover as directed and leave until all fermentation has ceased.

Blackcurrant and Rhubarb Appetizer

4 lb. rhubarb · 2 lb. blackcurrants
1 gallon water · 4 lb. sugar
champagne yeast · nutrient

Wipe the rhubarb sticks with a damp cloth and crush with a rolling pin, beginning in the middle and working with a rocking movement. Put the juice and pulp into six pints of water, add the crushed blackcurrants and leave to soak for twenty-four hours.

Strain, wring out dry and put the juice through a jelly-bag. Bring this juice to boiling-point and simmer for four minutes. Pour into the fermenting vessel and add half the sugar at once, stirring until all is dissolved. Allow to cool, then add the yeast starter and nutrient. Leave to ferment for ten days – covered as directed. Make a syrup of the rest of the sugar and water and add this to the bulk. Transfer to a jar, fit the fermentation lock or cover as directed and leave to ferment to completion.

Crab-Apple Table Wine

1 gallon crab-apples · 1 lb. raisins
1 gallon water · $3\frac{1}{2}$ lb. sugar
burgundy or tokay yeast · nutrient

Cut up the crab-apples as small as you can, or chop them if you can do it without chopping too many pips. Do not peel. Put them into six pints of water and leave to soak for twenty-four hours, stirring occasionally and crushing by hand if you can. They may be a bit hard to begin with.

Strain and wring out dry and put the juice through a jelly-bag. Bring the juice to boiling-point and simmer for five minutes. Pour into the fermenting vessel and add half the sugar at once, stirring until all is dissolved. Then add the chopped raisins. Allow to cool and add the yeast starter and nutrient. Cover as directed and ferment for ten days. Strain and wring out dry and add the rest of the sugar and water as syrup.

Transfer to a jar, fit the fermentation lock or cover as directed and leave until all fermentation has ceased.

BLACKCURRANT PORT

4 lb. blackcurrants • 3½ lb. sugar
1 gallon water • port yeast • nutrient

Crush the blackcurrants and pour six pints of cold water over them. Leave to soak for forty-eight hours.

Crush well, then strain and wring out dry and put the juice through a jelly-bag. Bring the juice to boiling-point and simmer for one minute. Pour the hot juice over half the sugar in the fermenting vessel and stir until all is dissolved. Allow to cool, then add the yeast starter and nutrient. Cover as directed and ferment for fourteen days. Make the rest of the water and sugar into a syrup and add this to the bulk.

Put into a jar and fit the fermentation lock or cover as directed and leave until all fermentation has ceased.

BLACKCURRANT TABLE WINE

3 lb. blackcurrants • 4 lb. sugar
1 gallon water • burgundy or tokay yeast
nutrient

Follow the directions given for Blackcurrant Port above.

Blackcurrant Light Dessert Wine

This is a dry wine that many people find most pleasing.

3 lb. blackcurrants • 3 lb. sugar
1 gallon water • sherry yeast • nutrient

Follow the directions given for Blackcurrant Port above.

Elderberry and Grape Port

3 lb. elderberries • 4 lb. black grapes
3½ lb. sugar • 1 gallon water • port yeast
nutrient

Crush both fruits and leave them to soak together overnight in six pints of water. Strain and wring out dry and put the juice through a jelly-bag. Bring this juice to boiling-point and simmer for three minutes. Pour the hot juice over half the sugar in the fermenting vessel and stir until all is dissolved. Allow to cool and then add the yeast starter and nutrient. Cover as directed and ferment for ten days. Then make a syrup of the rest of the sugar and water and add this to the bulk. Transfer to a jar and fit the fermentation lock or cover and leave until all fermentation has ceased.

Elderberry and Grape Burgundy

2½ lb. elderberries • 3 lb. green or amber grapes
3½ lb. sugar • burgundy yeast • nutrient
1 gallon water

Crush the two fruits together in one vessel and pour six pints of boiling water over them. Leave to soak for twelve hours. Strain and wring out dry and put this strained juice through a jelly-bag. Bring to boiling-point and simmer for two minutes. Pour this hot juice over half the sugar in the fermenting vessel and stir until all the sugar is dissolved.

When cool, add the yeast starter and nutrient. Cover as directed and ferment for ten days. Make a syrup of the rest of the sugar and water and add this to the bulk. Transfer to a jar and fit the fermentation lock or cover as directed and leave until all fermentation has ceased.

Damson Port

6–8 lb. damsons • 3½ lb. sugar
1 gallon water • port yeast • nutrient

Crush the damsons and pour six pints of cold water over them. Leave to soak overnight. Crush well and strain, wring out dry and put the juice through a jelly-bag. Damsons are loaded with pectin; therefore, thorough jelly-bag straining is essential – do not squeeze the bag. Bring the juice to boiling-point and simmer for three minutes. Pour the hot juice over half the sugar in the fermenting vessel and stir until all is dissolved. Allow to cool and add the yeast starter and nutrient.

Cover as advised and leave to ferment for ten days. Then make a syrup of the rest of the sugar and water and add this to the bulk. Transfer to a jar and fit the fermentation lock, or cover as directed and leave until all fermentation has ceased.

Whortleberry Port

4 – 5 lb. whortleberries • 4 lb. sugar
1 gallon water • port yeast • nutrient

Crush the berries and pour six pints of cold water over them. Leave to soak overnight. Strain and wring out dry and put the juice through a jelly-bag. Bring the strained juice to boiling-point and simmer for three minutes. Pour this hot juice over half the sugar in the fermenting vessel and stir until all the sugar is dissolved.

When cool add the yeast starter and nutrient. Cover as directed and leave to ferment for ten days.

Then make a syrup of the rest of the sugar and water and add this to the bulk. Transfer to a jar and fit the fermentation lock or cover as directed and leave until all fermentation has ceased.

Whortleberry Burgundy

3 lb. whortleberries • 3 lb. sugar
½ lb. raisins • 1 gallon water • burgundy yeast
nutrient

Follow the directions for Whortleberry Port, above, and ferment the chopped raisins for the ten days' fermentation period. Put the raisins in before the yeast is added. Straining after ten days will be necessary here.

Victoria Plum Port

This recipe is suitable for use with every variety of plum. Merely substitute for Victoria plums those available to you.

8 lb. plums • 3½ lb. sugar • 1 gallon water
port yeast • nutrient

Crush the plums and pour six pints of water over them. Leave to soak overnight. Strain and wring out dry and put the strained juice through a jelly-bag.

Bring the juice to boiling-point and simmer for five minutes. Pour the hot juice over half the sugar in the fermenting vessel, stirring until all the sugar is dissolved. When cool, add the yeast starter and nutrient. Cover as directed and ferment for ten days. Then add the rest of the sugar and water, in the form of a syrup, to the bulk. Transfer to a jar and fit the fermentation lock or cover as directed and leave until all fermentation ceases.

Plum Burgundy

Follow the directions for Plum Port, above, using:

6 lb. plums • 3 lb. sugar • 1 gallon water
burgundy yeast • nutrient

Mulberry Wine

Burgundy type.

5 pints mulberries • $3\frac{1}{2}$ lb. sugar
1 gallon water • burgundy yeast
nutrient

Note: Up to seven or even eight pints of fruit may be used without alteration to other ingredients.

Crush the fruits and pour six pints of boiling water over them. Leave to soak for twelve hours. Crush well and then strain; wring out dry and put the juice through a jelly-bag. Bring to the boil and simmer for three or four minutes. Pour into the fermenting vessel and add half the sugar, stirring until all is dissolved. Allow to cool and add the yeast starter and nutrient. Cover as directed and leave to ferment for ten days.

Then make a syrup of the rest of the water and sugar and add this to the bulk.

Transfer to a jar, fit the fermentation lock and leave to finish fermenting.

Loganberry Wine

5 pints loganberries • $3\frac{1}{2}$ lb. sugar
1 gallon water • burgundy yeast • nutrient

Crush the fruits and pour six pints of boiling water over them. Leave to soak for twenty-four hours, stirring often.

Crush well, then strain and wring out dry and put the juice through a jelly-bag. Bring the juice to boiling-point and simmer for three minutes. Pour into the fermenting vessel and add half the sugar, stirring until all is dissolved. When cool, add the yeast starter and nutrient. Cover as directed and ferment for fourteen days. Make the rest of the sugar and water into a syrup and put this in. Transfer to a jar and fit the fermentation lock or cover as directed and leave until all fermentation has ceased.

Raspberry Wine

6 lb. raspberries • 4 lb. sugar • 1 gallon water
malaga yeast • nutrient

Crush the fruits and pour six pints of boiling water over them. Leave to soak overnight. Crush well, strain, wring out dry and put the strained juice through a jelly-bag. Bring slowly to boiling-point and simmer for two minutes.

Pour into the fermenting vessel and add half the sugar, stirring until all is dissolved. Allow to cool, then add the yeast starter and nutrient. Cover as directed and ferment for ten days. Make the rest of the sugar and water into a syrup and add this to the bulk. Transfer to a jar and fit the fermentation lock or cover as directed and leave until all fermentation has ceased.

Raspberry Wine is often improved by adding a pound of dates as in the following recipe.

Raspberry and Date Wine

5 lb. raspberries • 1 lb. pressed (or loose) dates
3½ lb. sugar • 1 gallon water
burgundy yeast • nutrient

Follow the directions for Raspberry Wine, above, adding the cut-up dates before putting in the yeast.

Strain again before putting in the syrup and transferring to a jar.

Blackberry Wine

Port type.

> 6 lb. blackberries • 4 lb. sugar • 1 gallon water
> port yeast • nutrient

Crush the fruits and pour six pints of boiling water over them. Leave to soak overnight. Crush well and strain, wring out dry and put the strained juice through a jelly-bag. Bring slowly to the boil and simmer for three minutes. Pour into the fermenting vessel and add half the sugar, stirring until all is dissolved. Allow to cool and then add the yeast starter and nutrient. Cover as directed and ferment for fourteen days.

Make the rest of the sugar and water into a syrup and add this to the bulk. Transfer to a jar and fit the fermentation lock or cover as directed and leave until all fermentation has ceased.

Blackberry Burgundy

> 4 lb. blackberries • 3½ lb. sugar
> 1 gallon water • burgundy yeast
> nutrient

Proceed as for Blackberry Wine, above.

Orange Wine

It is quite a job to know how many oranges to recommend; different people like varying strengths of flavour so that I could advise as few as ten or as many as forty. I myself use twenty good-sized oranges and everybody tasting my orange wine thinks there's nothing quite like it. Let's say twenty, then, shall we? This will be quite strongly flavoured, so fifteen fair-sized oranges could be used, with excellent results, to one gallon of water, four pounds of sugar, all-purpose wine yeast and nutrient. Cut up the oranges and peel quite small and crush them well, but do not crush the pips. Pour four pints of water over them; leave to soak for forty-eight hours, crushing as often as you like during that time. Strain and wring out dry, bring this strained juice just to boiling-point and cut off the heat at once.

Take half the sugar and a quart of water; boil the water and dissolve the sugar in it and add this to the rest. This should now be cool enough to add the yeast starter at once – but don't forget to add the nutrient. Cover as directed and ferment for ten days. Then make a syrup of the two pounds of sugar and quart of water and add this to the rest. Transfer to a jar, fit fermentation lock or cover as directed and leave until all fermentation has ceased.

Tangerine and Orange Special

A very special wine may be made from a mixture of tangerines and oranges. I know several people who save a couple of their Christmas tangerines and all the peel from those eaten and make a very good wine from these with just a couple of oranges added. The proportions I recommend and can vouch for are: ten fair-sized oranges, eight tangerines, four pounds of sugar, one gallon of water, all-purpose wine yeast and nutrient.

Cut both fruits (including the peel) very small and pour six pints of boiling water over them. Crush and squeeze as much as you can and as often as you like during the following forty-eight hours. Strain and wring out dry and put the juice through a jelly-bag. Jelly-bag straining is not so essential here because we shall not be boiling the juice, but it does help the wine to clear. Take a quart of the strained juice and warm it just enough to dissolve half the sugar in it. When this is dissolved add the yeast starter and nutrient.

Cover as directed and ferment for ten days. Then make the rest of the sugar and water into a syrup and add this to the bulk. Transfer to a jar, fit the fermentation lock or cover as directed and leave until all fermentation has ceased.

For Your Own Recipes

For Your Own Recipes

17

Dried Fruit Wines the Modern Way

Surprisingly good wines may be made from dried fruits, especially when a wine yeast is used. These wines usually need a little acid put into them, because they lack this essential part of the flavour. The reader need have no fear that the wine will be flavoured of the lemons or oranges or whatever is used – the number used is not enough to flavour the wine. But the acid contained in them is enough to bring out other flavours.

Many people like to add a teaspoonful of tea as well, but I have not yet found the need for this. My liking may be different from others', so readers who think that a little tannin would be an advantage may add a teaspoonful of tea to the gallon just before adding the yeast.

In the following recipes we begin with nine pints of water; this is important, for it makes up for loss during boiling. Dried fruits have no juice whereas fresh fruits have – so don't forget that extra pint.

RAISIN WINE

3 lb. raisins · 3 lemons · 2 lb. sugar
9 pints water · all-purpose wine yeast
nutrient

Chop the raisins and pour seven pints of boiling water over them. Leave to soak for twenty-four hours, crushing well with the hands during this time.

Then strain through fine muslin and squeeze in the juice of the lemons. Bring just to boiling-point and simmer for two minutes. Pour the hot liquid over half the sugar in the fermenting vessel and stir until all the sugar is dissolved. Allow to cool and then add the yeast starter and nutrient. Ferment for ten days – covered as directed, of course. Then make the rest of the water and sugar into a syrup and add this to the bulk.

Transfer to a jar and fit the fermentation lock or cover as directed and leave until all fermentation has ceased.

Currant Wine

4 lb. currants • 2 lemons • 2 oranges
2½ lb. sugar • 9 pints water
all-purpose wine yeast • nutrient

Bring seven pints of water just to boiling-point and put in the currants. Cut off the heat at once. Leave the mixture to soak for forty-eight hours, but crush with the hands as much and as often as you like during that time.

Strain through fine muslin, bring the strained juice to boiling-point and simmer for three minutes. Pour the hot liquid over half the sugar in the fermenting vessel and stir until all is dissolved, then squeeze in the juice of the lemons. Allow to cool and add the yeast starter and nutrient.

Cover as directed and ferment for ten days. Make a syrup of the rest of the sugar and the other quart of water and add this to the rest. Transfer to a jar and fit the fermentation lock or cover as directed and leave to finish fermenting.

Prune Wine

4 lb. prunes • ½ lb. raisins or sultanas
2 lemons • 2½ lb. sugar • all-purpose wine yeast
nutrient • 9 pints water

Bring seven pints of water to the boil and pour in the prunes. Cut off the heat at once. Leave to soak for forty-eight hours. During this time crush well and as often as you like – the more the better.

Strain through fine muslin and bring the juice to boiling-point. Pour the hot liquid over half the sugar in the fermenting vessel. Stir until all the sugar is dissolved and then add the chopped raisins and the juice of the lemons.

Allow to cool, then add the yeast starter and nutrient. Cover as directed and ferment for ten days. Strain and add the rest of the sugar and water in the form of a syrup.

Transfer to a jar and fit the fermentation lock or cover as directed and leave until all fermentation has ceased.

Dried-Apricot Wine

6 lb. dried apricots · 1 orange · 1 lemon
9 pints water · 3½ lb. sugar
all-purpose wine yeast · nutrient

Bring seven pints of water to the boil and put in the apricots. Cut off the heat at once. Leave to soak for forty-eight hours and crush well and often during this time.

Crush thoroughly once more and strain through fine muslin. Bring the juice to boiling-point and simmer for five minutes. Pour the hot liquid over half the sugar and stir until all the sugar is dissolved. Then squeeze in the juice of the orange and lemon.

When cool, add the yeast starter and nutrient. Cover as directed and ferment for ten days. Make the rest of the sugar and water into a syrup and add this to the bulk. Transfer to a jar and fit the fermentation lock or cover as directed and leave until all fermentation has ceased.

Date Wine

3 lb. dates (packeted or loose) • 3 oranges
3 lemons • 9 pints water • 2 lb. sugar
all-purpose wine yeast • nutrient

Cut up the dates very finely and put them into seven pints of boiling water. Leave them until the water reaches boiling-point again and cut off the heat at once. Leave to soak for twelve hours, stirring occasionally. Strain through fine muslin and bring the juice just to boiling-point. Pour this over half the sugar and stir until all is dissolved. Then squeeze in the juice of the oranges and lemons. Allow to cool and add the yeast starter and nutrient.

Cover as directed and ferment for seven days. Make the rest of the sugar and water into a syrup and add this to the bulk. Transfer to a jar and fit the fermentation lock or cover as directed and leave until all fermentation has ceased.

Prune, Raisin and Sultana Wine

2 lb. prunes • 1 lb. raisins • ½ lb. sultanas
2 oranges • 2½ lb. sugar • 9 pints water
all-purpose wine yeast • nutrient

Cut the prunes in half and remove the stones. Put the stoned prunes with the chopped raisins and sultanas into seven pints of water and bring just to boiling-point. Cut off the heat at once. Leave to soak for twelve hours and then crush well with the hands. Strain through fine muslin and bring the juice to boiling-point. Pour this over half the sugar and stir until all is dissolved. Then squeeze in the juice of the oranges. When cool add the yeast starter and nutrient.

Cover as directed and ferment for ten days. Then make a syrup of the rest of the sugar and water and add this to the bulk. Transfer to a jar and fit the fermentation lock or cover as directed and leave until all fermentation has ceased.

Currant, Sultana and Prune Wine

2 lb. currants • 1 lb. sultanas • 1 lb. prunes
3 lemons • 2½ lb. sugar • 9 pints water
all-purpose wine yeast • nutrient

This recipe is worked to the directions given for Prune, Raisin and Sultana Wine, above.

For Your Own Recipes

For Your Own Recipes

18

Root Wines the Modern Way

A satisfactory ferment is more important with potato wines and wine made from ingredients containing starch, such as roots, wheat and rice, than with other wines. By this I do not mean that a satisfactory ferment is not important with fruit wines; of course it is. But it is even more important if we want wines made with starchy materials to become perfectly clear.

Many people complain that the starch boiled into the water at the beginning remains in the finished wine, and that efforts to clarify with isinglass and egg-white only make matters worse. Filtering the wine, they say, has practically no effect, and ruins the flavour in any case. There is no point in filtering the potato water or whatever it is before making the wine, because no method of filtering will remove dissolved starch. In that case, they ask, why does potato wine clear at all? The answer lies in a satisfactory ferment.

Yeast converts starch to sugar and thence to alcohol. A weak yeast will be 'smothered' if too much sugar is added at the beginning; it is therefore unable to convert the starch to sugar, and leaves it in suspension in the wine, which becomes cloudy.

Almost everyone – including myself – has for years put all the sugar in at the start and never had a clearing problem until a poor yeast was used. Most people are still using bakers' yeast, and probably many will never use anything else; quite likely they will never have a clearing problem to deal with. But it is better not to take risks, for there are plenty of poor yeasts about.

If you must still use bakers' yeast, make sure it is fresh and use a nutrient or a specially prepared yeast food; this will put plenty of 'guts' into yeast if it happens to be lacking in any.

All this may lead you to think that, because we add some of the sugar at the start and more later on, wine yeasts are weak. This is not so; wine yeasts are different from bakers' yeast and do not like to be overworked. They are not weak, they merely like to do their job slowly and efficiently.

In the following recipes I have specified 'yeast' without naming any special kind. This is so that readers may use an all-purpose wine yeast, an ordinary dried yeast in 'pellet' form – these incidentally are often very vigorous – or, if you still insist, bakers' yeast.

It should be borne in mind that wheat and raisins added when the brew has cooled will not be sterilized during the process. Because these may be carrying all sorts of harmful bacteria that can spoil the wine, it is a good plan to scald them well before adding them to the brew. Alternatively, dissolve one Campden tablet in three pints of water in a non-metal container and drop the wheat and *whole* raisins (not cut up) into this. Then strain them at once through a polythene colander or cloth and pour some boiled water over them to rid them of the sulphur dioxide.

If oranges and lemons are to be used, treat them the same way: this should be done before cutting them up.

Parsnip Wine

4 lb. parsnips · 1 lb. raisins · 1 lb. kibbled maize
2 oranges · 2 lemons · 3½ lb. sugar
9 pints water · yeast

Scrub, grate or mince the parsnips and put them in seven pints of water. Bring slowly to boiling-point and simmer for five minutes, taking off all scum that rises.

Strain through two thicknesses of fine muslin (or a strong, coarse cloth) and add half the sugar, stirring until all is dissolved. Then add the maize, the raisins and the juice of the oranges and lemons. Allow to cool, then add the yeast and nutrient or yeast food – not both. Cover as directed and ferment for ten to fourteen days, stirring daily and crushing the raisins by hand at least three times during the fourteen-day period. Strain and wring out fairly dry. Make a syrup of the rest of the sugar and water and add this to the bulk.

Transfer to a jar and fit the fermentation lock or cover as directed and leave until all fermentation has ceased.

Potato Wine

3 lb. potatoes · ½ lb. raisins · ½ lb. dates
1 lb. wheat or kibbled maize · 2 oranges
2 lemons · 4 lb. sugar · 9 pints water
yeast · nutrient or yeast food

Proceed as for Parsnip Wine, above.

Beetroot Wine

4 lb. beetroots · 3 lemons · ½ lb. raisins
3½ lb. sugar · 9 pints water
yeast and nutrient or yeast food

Proceed as for Parsnip Wine, page 150, but simmer the beetroots for ten minutes.

Carrot Wine

The only reason the trade does not make a wine from carrots for sale to the general public is that it feels that people would not buy it simply because it happens to be made of carrots. But I will bet my last bottle of ten-year-old carrot whisky that they will one day do this –

and charge about eight and six a bottle for it. We can make it for eight bob less than that.

>   5 lb. carrots · ½ lb. raisins · ½ lb. kibbled maize
>   2 oranges · 2 lemons · 4 lb. sugar
>   9 pints water · yeast and nutrient or yeast food

Proceed as for Parsnip Wine, page 150, but simmer the carrots for fifteen minutes.

Norah's Favourite

>   3 lb. carrots · 2 lb. potatoes · 1 lb. raisins
>   2 oranges · 2 lemons · 3½ lb sugar
>   9 pints water · yeast and nutrient

My wife prefers this wine made with bakers' yeast and nutrient. But there is nothing to prevent you using the yeast of your choice. Scrub, grate and mince the carrots and potatoes. Put them in the water and simmer gently for ten minutes, taking off all scum that rises. Strain into the fermenting vessel and add half the sugar, stirring until all is dissolved. Then add the chopped raisins and cut-up oranges and peel.

Allow to cool and add the yeast and nutrient. Cover as directed and ferment for ten days. During this time take the oranges and lemons and squeeze them well at least three times; stir up the raisins at the same time. After ten days, strain and wring out dry.

Make a syrup of the rest of the sugar and water and add this to the bulk. Transfer to a jar and fit the fermentation lock or cover as directed and leave until all fermentation has ceased.

For Your Own Recipes

For Your Own Recipes

19
Champagne and Sparkling Wines

Certain writers on wine-making (who should have known better) have concluded some of their recipes with the words: 'This will make a lovely sparkling wine.' They also call certain of their recipes 'So-and-so Champagne'. The directions they give are the same as those for making any other sort of wine; the result, therefore, cannot be a champagne unless it happens by an accident not allowed for in the recipe. What probably happened is that these 'experts' once made a sparkling wine by accident, and not knowing how or why it had happened, simply attributed the effervescence to one of the ingredients and passed the recipe on to their public as champagne.

As we all know, champagne is made from grapes; anything resembling champagne made from fruit other than grapes must then be termed 'sparkling wine', and considerable experience is needed before these can be made satisfactorily and without accident. In the early stages proceed as with any other wine, putting the wine under fermentation locks after fourteen days' fermentation. But instead of allowing the wine to ferment itself out, watch carefully until fermentation has *almost* ceased; at this stage the wine should be carefully bottled with as little lees as possible.

Great care must be taken from now on, for our aim is to seal the bottles while the champagne is still fermenting. If we seal them too soon the result will be a series of explosions – and curses upon my head – and if we seal them too late we shall merely produce a wine with a weak sparkle that will expend itself in a few minutes, leaving behind it a still wine.

I have chosen this method for readers of this book for I do believe it to be the simplest. Another method calls for the addition of sugar to a blend of wines already made and matured. A yeast capable of withstanding the amount of alcohol in the blend is then introduced and fermentation allowed to go on in sealed containers, such as stone jars with the bungs wired on.

By using the method I recommend here, the reader has far greater hope of success, for he will be able to decide when fermentation has almost ceased and seal the bottles at the best time. Very strong bottles are needed; those used for aerated waters are excellent for our purpose for not only are they very strong but they have screw stoppers. Ordinary corks present an almost insurmountable difficulty for the inexperienced champagne-maker.

When the still-fermenting champagne is put into bottles fermentation may become very vigorous; if this happens, allow the fermentation to slow down before screwing home the stoppers. Fermentation will continue – despite the absence of air – and the carbon-dioxide gas will be absorbed into the wine.

When fermentation has ceased the champagne will deposit its lees and slowly become clear. And this is where our troubles begin. Opening the bottles to re-bottle the clear champagne releases the gas, with the result that the lees rise up into the wine. It is a waste of time to screw down the stopper and wait for the wine to clear, for subsequent openings will meet with the same result until all the gas has been given off and has left behind it a still wine.

Our method, then, must be as follows. While the champagne is clearing, the bottles must be stood upside down in a partitioned cardboard crate. This will protect each bottle if by accident the stoppers have been screwed up too soon and one bottle happens to explode. This should not happen if strong bottles are used. If the bottles are stood upside down the lees settle on the stopper; the amount of lees present at this stage will depend on the care taken at the bottling and should not be more than one-eighth of an inch.

Now comes the real difficulty.

Carefully and very gently, and while the bottles are still held upside down, unscrew the stopper. It need only be turned a little way to allow the compressed carbon-dioxide gas to squirt out the lees. As soon as the lees have gone, screw up the stopper. (You can practise this with a bottle of aerated water.)

By using screw stoppers (screw caps are not suitable) the risk of the gas forcing the stopper right out, as would most certainly happen if ordinary corks were used, is eliminated.

My father tried to teach me the art of releasing the lees in this way, but always the cork forced itself out, to the accompaniment of growls from one with no patience for the incompetent. He used ordinary corks wired on, and I still marvel today at the ease with which he removed the wire, released the lees and wired on the cork again with never an accident.

Do not attempt to remove the lees until the champagne is crystal-clear, otherwise a second go will be necessary with perhaps too much loss of the gas essential to a sparkling wine.

Rhubarb 'Champagne'

8 lb. rhubarb · 5 lb. sugar
1 gallon water · yeast

Use baker's yeast if you wish, or use wine yeast according to the instructions of the supplier.

Remove leaves and stumps, wipe the sticks clean with a damp cloth and then proceed with the method of your choice.

Blackcurrant 'Champagne'

4 lb. blackcurrants • 3½ lb. sugar
1 gallon water • yeast

Strip the fruits from the stalks and then proceed with the method of your choice.

Green Gooseberry 'Champagne'

3–4 quarts gooseberries
4–5 lb. sugar according to the amount of fruit being used
1 gallon water • yeast

Crush the fruits and proceed with the method of your choice.

Apple 'Champagne'

6 or 7 lb. firm, ripe, juicy fruit of any variety except cooking apples
4 lb. sugar • 1 gallon water • yeast

If a press is not available the apples will have to be grated and then chopped. Do not peel or core them. Proceed with the method of your choice.

Pear 'Champagne'

8 lb. reasonably sweet and juicy pears which must be firm and ripe
4 lb. sugar • 1 gallon water • yeast

Crush the fruit if possible; if no press is available they should be grated. Do not peel or core. Proceed with the method of your choice.

CHAMPAGNE AND SPARKLING WINES

As will be seen, any wine may be turned into a sparkling wine merely by following the method outlined above. Readers who fancy that their favourite fruit or root wine would be improved by being made as a sparkling wine will now know what to do.

I must repeat my warning that considerable experience is needed before one is able to decide when fermentation has almost ceased and the time is ripe for screwing home the stoppers. The strong bottles I have recommended will withstand immense pressure, so the risk of explosion is not great. I have been using this method, and the bottles recommended, for many years without mishap.

For Your Own Recipes

For Your Own Recipes

20

Sugar, Acid and Alcohol

The actual composition, in exact quantities, of any given fruit is a variable unknown; even if it could be precisely determined it would not be the same in two consecutive seasons. Soil, situation, weather, type of tree, all have something to do with it. Even fruit of the same variety, grown under apparently identical conditions, would be found upon analysis to vary in their percentages of known elements.

Commercial producers are aware of this inconsistency; the grapes they grow on the same vines in the same soil are not identical in two consecutive seasons.

One might well ask – if this is true, how can two bottles of the same wine bought perhaps a year apart taste the same? Those two bottles of wine that seem the same may not be really; one may contain only two different wines whilst the other may contain many more. One can well imagine the patience and skill needed to blend several wines so that the result contains the characteristics that have made that particular brand popular.

Where home-grown fruit is being made into wine by the grower, he will think to himself, 'Well, it's been a dryish summer with plenty of sun; this means that there will be more sugar in the fruit this year.' There will be less sugar in fruit following a poor summer that has been rather wet. Accordingly he will adjust the amount of sugar by an ounce or so per pound of fruit used. Alternatively, he will follow the recipe to the letter and will not mind if there is a slight variation in two wines

SUGAR, ACID AND ALCOHOL

turned out with the same fruit and the same recipe. Obviously, if we use six pounds of fruit in one gallon of water we shall have slightly more sugar (fruit sugar) in the mixture than if we use only four pounds of fruit. And if the summer has been dry there will be more sugar than if it had been wet.

Since the sweetness or acidity of fruit can vary so much from year to year, obviously if you want to produce the same result each time from the same recipe you must have some means of ascertaining the extent of the variation. This is where the hydrometer comes in. But first a word about sugar and acid.

The following table is not complete, but it is sufficient to show the reader that each fruit contains varied amounts of sugar and that the sugar content of each fruit varies quite a bit. The table, which may come in handy to those who want to experiment with using a hydrometer, is based on fruits grown under normal soil and weather conditions.

Fruit	Sugar content %
Blackcurrants	7–8$\frac{1}{2}$
Gooseberries	3$\frac{1}{2}$–7
Strawberries	5–7$\frac{1}{2}$
Cherries	7$\frac{1}{2}$–12
Redcurrants	3–7
Whitecurrants	4$\frac{1}{2}$–5$\frac{1}{2}$
Blackberries	5$\frac{1}{2}$–6$\frac{1}{2}$
Raspberries	4$\frac{1}{2}$–8
Loganberries	4$\frac{1}{2}$–7
Apples	9–14$\frac{1}{2}$
Plums	4$\frac{1}{2}$–12

Different varieties of apples and plums might well contain amounts of sugar varying slightly from those above.

It is interesting to take gooseberries and strawberries as an example of how misleading one's palate can be when relied upon to compare the sugar contained in two different fruits. One might well suppose that strawberries contain ten times more sugar than gooseberries, and to say: 'Well, then, gooseberries *must* contain more acid.' They do, in fact, but the difference is not so great as you would think.

The following table gives the approximate acid content of some fruits grown under normal soil and weather conditions.

Fruit	*Acid content %*
Blackcurrants	$1\frac{1}{2}$–3
Gooseberries	1–$1\frac{1}{2}$ (possibly $1\frac{3}{4}$)
Strawberries	$\frac{1}{4}$–1 (possibly $1\frac{1}{4}$)
Cherries	$1\frac{1}{4}$–$1\frac{3}{4}$
Redcurrants	$1\frac{1}{4}$–3
Whitecurrants	$1\frac{1}{2}$–3
Blackberries	$\frac{1}{4}$–2
Raspberries	$1\frac{1}{4}$–$2\frac{1}{2}$ (possibly $2\frac{3}{4}$)
Loganberries	$1\frac{1}{4}$–2
Apples	$\frac{1}{2}$–$1\frac{1}{2}$
Plums	$\frac{1}{2}$–$1\frac{3}{4}$

From the sugar table it will be obvious that, because we shall be diluting our juices, the actual amount of fruit sugar in the mixture will be very small indeed, and may, for all practical purposes, be disregarded for the time being. The acid content should be about right.

Now let us take grapes. Grapes, both black and white (and presumably those we call 'amber'), contain from fifteen to thirty-three per cent (possibly thirty-five per cent) of sugar. Because grape juice is rarely diluted a great deal, we must not overlook this high percentage of sugar. Nor must we overlook that gap between fifteen and thirty-three per cent.

It is here that the hydrometer comes in handy. Many people would call it essential, but I cannot agree: I have grown grapes and made good wine from them without a hydrometer. Yet I have found it useful, for it allows one to ascertain the exact amount of sugar contained in a must, so that the user can start with the same amount in consecutive brews.

Now, how much sugar should a must contain? Actually, there is no 'right' amount. Each type of wine will need a different amount of sugar; and even if the 'right' amount of sugar is in the must at the outset to produce that particular wine-type, it must not be overlooked that your own care, the extent of yeast action (one can never be absolutely certain at what point the yeast will stop working) and other factors bear upon the finished product.

In order to ascertain and control the amount of sugar in your must – the 'specific gravity' – you need a simple and inexpensive instrument, the hydrometer. This consists of a glass or plastic flask and a weighted float with a long, thin stem on which are marked the readings to be taken. A sample of the strained juice (or a specially strained sample if you are fermenting on the skins) is poured into the flask. This should be warmed slowly to 60°F, and the float is then gently put in and allowed to float freely. The point where the stem sticks out of the liquid indicates the gravity of the must. Remember, however, when you are using a hydrometer, to take into account the surface tension of the juice. Where the stem sticks out of the liquid (see Fig. 3) the surrounding liquid climbs a little way up it. The reading should be taken where the liquid would have cut the stem if there had been no surface tension – i.e. you should ignore that slight rise just around the stem.

The gravity of water is 1·000 (often written simply as 1·). Our juices, even though diluted, will give a reading above this figure. How much higher will depend on the amount of sugar contained in the must. In the case of grape juice the ideal gravity would seem to be 1·100; in a good year this reading might be attained without the addition of sugar.

A point to bear in mind here is that the decimal point is quite often dropped, so that a reading of 1150 is really 1·150. The more usual practice, however, is to drop the 1· and refer, for instance, to a reading of 1·110 as 'a gravity of 110'. This practice is now becoming general, and I myself always refer to my musts as having a gravity of 100 or 110 or 125 or whatever it may be.

When wine is made from fruits other than grapes there are other points to bear in mind; the main one being that we shall not be fermenting the pure juice or even a juice diluted only very little. More likely we shall be diluting our juices to as little as perhaps one-sixth of their original gravity – not to get more from our fruits but because it might be quite unpalatable if we did not. Naturally we want a nice wine, one well flavoured of the fruit we are using and one with a comfortable percentage of alcohol. But we do not want one so devoid of sweetness that when we sample it our tongues roll up, our cheeks cave in and our faces appear to be caught up in a vice.

Therefore, apart from using sufficient sugar to give the percentage of alcohol we want, we must also allow for some unfermented sugar to remain in the wine to sweeten it. It will be found that my recipes allow for just that, but since the amount of sugar in the fruit will vary from season to season, only with a hydrometer can you be sure that the must will always be the same.

A hydrometer reading from 1·000 to 1·200 is best for the home wine-maker, for it allows him to take the gravity of musts above the 1·100 mark. And since he will want musts containing sufficient sugar to produce about fourteen per cent of alcohol by volume and still

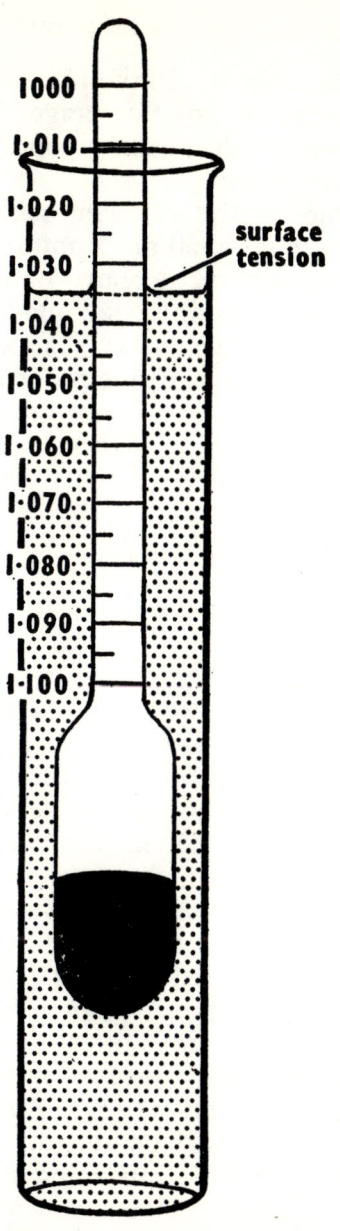

3. *The Hydrometer, showing how to allow for surface tension.*

have a little sugar left in the finished wine, he will need a hydrometer covering this range. Alternatively, he can use two, one reading from 1·000 to 1·100 and another reading from 1·100 to 1·200.

Let us look at the following table. This is not complete, because we shall not want a wine containing less than nine per cent of alcohol, and it is unlikely that we shall be able to produce one above fourteen per cent, which is plenty (remember that we are talking about alcohol by volume and not proof spirit).

Specific Gravity	Potential Alcohol %
1070	9·0
1080	10·5
1090	11·9
1100	13·4
1110	14·5

Now, let us suppose we have taken the gravity of a must to which no sugar has yet been added and that the gravity is 1070. This would give us a wine containing nine per cent of alcohol. We decide that this is not enough and wish to make a wine of fourteen per cent. Therefore we must add some sugar.

Here it is useful to remember that two and a quarter ounces of sugar added to one gallon of must raises the hydrometer reading by roughly five degrees. As we want to raise it from 1070 to 1110—raise it forty degrees—we calculate: 'Five into forty goes eight times, so eight times two and a quarter ounces, or eighteen ounces, of sugar must be added.'

It may well be that a must containing as yet no added sugar might give a reading as low as 1020. In this event the reader may make a rapid calculation to find how much sugar is needed to raise it to 1110.

If we add just enough sugar to produce the amount of alcohol we want, the resulting wine will most likely be dry, since all the sugar will have been fermented out. This is a useful point to remember when a dry wine is required.

The amount of sugar that must remain in the wine to give it just that pleasant sweetness will depend on the palate of the individual maker, and he must calculate for himself, taking into consideration the type of fruit he is using.

The best plan for the beginner is to use a recipe and to take the gravity of the must (fruit-juice and water mixture) before adding the first lot of sugar. From this he will know how much sugar is needed to bring the gravity up to the point that will produce the amount of alcohol he wants. Having done this he will add the sugar needed and then allow fermentation to go on. After fourteen days he will add the second lot of sugar and take the reading again – making a note of each. As fermentation progresses he will take weekly (or more frequent) readings. When fermentation has ceased he will be able to judge whether slightly more or slightly less sugar should have been added.

When taking the gravity of musts that are fermenting, it is wise to shake the sample gently to release the carbon dioxide bubbles contained in it and to give the hydrometer a twist so that any bubbles clinging to it are also released. If this is not done, gross inaccuracies may occur. But for heaven's sake don't be afraid of the hydrometer: you will be surprised how ridiculously easy it is to use and understand. Once you have mastered it you will never regret it.

How Strong is My Wine?

Every home wine-maker wants a reasonably accurate answer to that question; and provided he is satisfied with reasonable accuracy he can test his wine at home and not be more than an unimportant point or two either side of precision.

On the other hand, if he cannot be satisfied, he will have to submit samples to test at a laboratory – or perhaps his chemist will test his wine for him. Either way he will have to pay, for testing involves distilling; and since two batches of wine are likely to vary in their alcoholic content, each would have to undergo a test.

The home wine-maker should not be tempted to distil a sample, for if he did he might well find that he has also distilled for himself a prison sentence (see pp. 86–87).

I do not propose to tell you how to distil; just let me say that when a sample has been distilled, this distillate is made up with distilled water and the gravity taken at 60°F. The reading is then compared with tables giving the percentages of proof-spirit against the relative specific gravities.

In the following table, which is not complete, the reader will note that the readings are below the 1·000 mark.

Specific gravity	Proof-spirit (%)
0·995	5·98
0·996	4·73
0·997	3·52
0·998	2·33
0·999	1·16

Note that the lower the reading the higher the proof-spirit – up to a certain limit.

Home testing with an instrument known as the vinometer is quite simple; and since this is one of the most interesting aspects of wine-making, the reader should

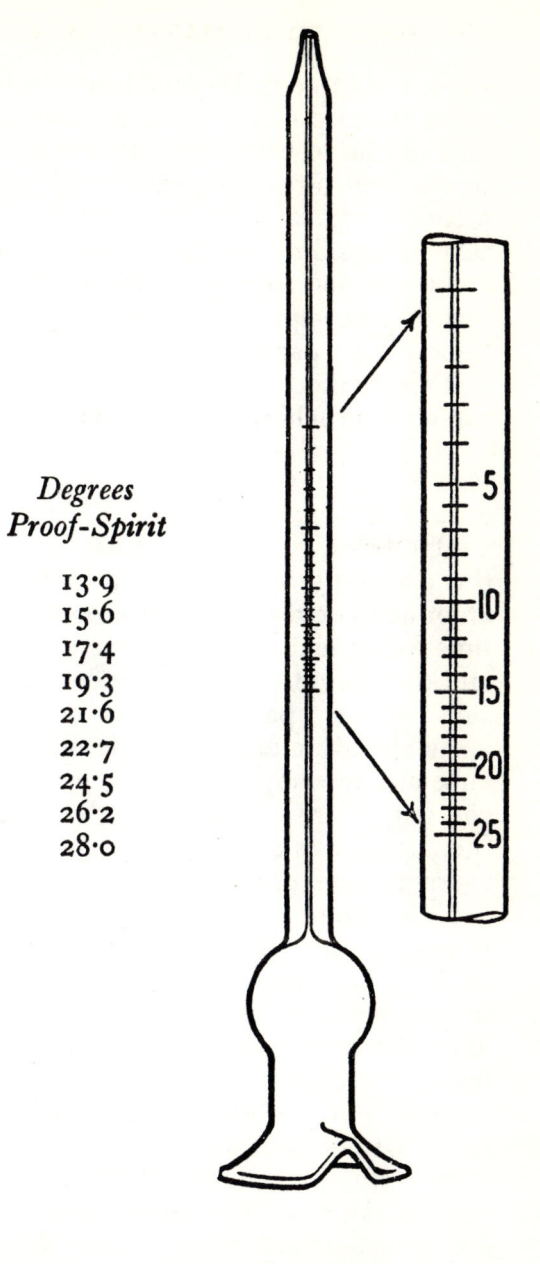

Alcohol by Vol. (%)	Degrees Proof-Spirit
8	13·9
9	15·6
10	17·4
11	19·3
12	21·6
13	22·7
14	24·5
15	26·2
16	28·0

4. The Vinometer, and some readings.

have a vinometer in preference to some other refinement of equipment. It is quite inexpensive (about 7s. 6d.) and simple to use; full instructions are sent with each instrument. Broadly speaking, all one has to do is to put a couple of drops of wine into the vinometer and then turn it upside down and take the reading. This will show the percentage of alcohol by volume. To arrive at the proof-spirit content compare the reading with the table on page 167.

This method does not give complete accuracy, which can only be achieved by distillation.

Balance of Acid

One often hears the phrase 'correct acidity'. From the chemist's point of view there may be a 'correct' amount of acid to have in a must at the outset or in a finished wine, but personal tastes are what matter most, and the skill in wine-making comes in making wines to suit your own palate.

As already mentioned, one needs laboratory experience and test apparatus to determine correctly the acid content of fruit juices and the musts prepared from them, and this is likely to be beyond the scope of the average home producer. Nor is it necessary.

If we were going to ferment the pure juices, or juices diluted, say, by a quarter or half, we would need to determine the acid content – especially if the fruits we happened to be using were known to be rather high in acid – and adjust it. But our juices, and therefore the acid present, will be diluted to such an extent that the possibility of there being too much acid present in the must does not arise.

Nevertheless, many people who are fond of rhubarb wine admit that they would like it even more were it not for its acidity.

The oxalic acid in a must prepared from rhubarb is

easily removed with pure medicinal chalk (precipitated chalk) obtainable from chemists. A quarter to half an ounce (not more) is worked into a smooth paste – a teaspoonful of must in a cup is ideal for this – and then stirred into the bulk. As it may take some time for the crystallized acid to settle, it is best to go ahead with making the wine as the acid crystals will be left behind in the lees at the first racking; this in most cases is at the fourteen-days stage. If the operator is not using Campden tablets and proposes to boil the juice, he will have to strain it first through two or three thicknesses of fine muslin to remove the acid particles.

One often hears of a wine being sharp, but otherwise a very pleasant drink, and that sweetening with sugar, although it improves matters, does not have the effect desired; there is still some sharpness, though this is less 'biting'. It is a common belief that sugar will neutralize the acid in a fruit juice or wine. This is not so. Raw rhubarb or lemon dipped in sugar will still shrivel one's tongue; the same will apply, only a little less so, in a must or finished wine. You can apply the de-acidification technique to a finished wine if you wish, with precipitated chalk as described above, but I have found that the flavour of the wine is usually impaired.

The remedy most easily applied is that of blending an acid wine with a non-acid wine. For example, if a wine is too acid and sugar makes no satisfactory difference, the best plan is to blend it with a dried-fruit wine; these are usually lower in acid than other wines unless rather more acid than usual was added at the outset. Dried-fruit wines made with the recipes in this book will be low in acid and therefore ideal for blending with an acid wine.

The alternative to this is to use dates or raisins; one pound of either to a gallon of must prepared from fruits known to produce wines that are slightly 'tart', will put matters right.

21
Some Questions and Answers

RHUBARB WINE

I am making my rhubarb wine as an ordinary wine, fermenting it in the tub. I cannot decide whether it is fermenting properly: there is no froth on the surface of the brew, instead the surface looks something like drizzle on a puddle. Do you think it is working properly?

Working well. Not all fruit wines froth during fermentation, and those that do usually cease to do so after a day or so. The surface of the brew would then appear as you have described it.

SWEETENING FINISHED WINES

My wine is perfectly clear, being nearly a year old, but it is rather too sharp. Will sweetening with sugar bring about more fermentation?

If, as you say, your wine is perfectly clear and reasonably old, sweetening with sugar will not begin another ferment, simply because the alcoholic volume is too great to allow this. In other words, there is no live yeast present to work upon the sugar you intend to sweeten your wine with. First siphon it, using sterilized tubing, off any lees that may happen to be in the bottle and then warm it a little, very slowly, in a covered vessel which has also been sterilized. Add the amount of sugar you think will be sufficient – one or two teaspoonfuls per bottle should be ample. Stir this in until all is dissolved and then bottle again in sterilized bottles and seal with sterilized corks. Remember that screw-tops cannot be too tightly screwed down.

It might perhaps be best to label your bottles – 'needs sweetening' – and then sweeten each bottle as it is required for use. Do not allow the wine to become hot, as the alcohol may be driven off and might easily catch fire. This has happened to one of my own brews.

White sugar will not cloud the wine.

Adding Wheat and Raisins

May I add wheat and raisins to all the wines I make? I have been very successful so far with my wine-making, but I am anxious to do even better. . . .

This is a question I frequently have to answer: always with the same words – it is for you to decide. However, I would advise you not to use raisins when making flower wines: these wines have an 'aromatic' flavour (I cannot otherwise describe it) which raisins might very well spoil. Raisins are best used in wines which are inclined to be 'thin' without them. By 'thin', in this instance, I mean lacking in body. The best examples I can give of this are that expensive port is full-bodied, while cheap port-style wines are 'thin'.

Certain fruit wines, such as red currant and raspberry, though excellent wines, are sometimes improved by the addition of say half a pound or a pound of raisins per gallon. The raisins should be added to the brew when all the sugar is dissolved and before the yeast is added.

It must be stressed that to add raisins or wheat to recipes that do not call for them is strictly a matter of choice, and I would advise you to make the wines first without raisins, and then with; you may then decide which you prefer. In any case, another point must be watched if raisins are used when not called for: there is the risk of producing a wine of too high a specific gravity – a liquid containing too much minute solids per ratio of water.

Half a pound or a pound of wheat may be added to most wines (except flower wines), but I have found that it is chiefly root wines which benefit from this addition.

Hops in Wine

A friend tells me that he always uses hops when making wine, but he will not tell me how to use them. Hops grow at the end of my garden; if these may be used in wine-making, will you please tell me the best way to use them?

Unfortunately, hops are available to only a few of us, and those who can get them are indeed lucky. Root wines are improved greatly by the addition of a few hops but do not use them in fruit or flower wines, or those which call for the addition of wheat and raisins.

First gather the hops when they are ripe and dry – put them in a paper bag and hang in a dry cupboard. One teacupful of hops per gallon of brew is the usual ratio, and the hops are boiled with the roots. Rub the hops through the hands before measuring them, and do not pack them down into the cup.

Various firms supplying wine-makers' requirements supply malt and hop mixtures (dried); many people like to add about two ounces of this mixture to their root wines in the same way as hops.

If readers who have difficulty in locating supplies of dried malt and hops care to get in touch with me through my publishers (stamped addressed envelope, please!), I shall be happy to advise them.

Testing for Clarity

I would like to test my wine for clarity; is there any way of doing this other than tapping the cask?

Wines should not be repeatedly tapped for sampling; frequent opening invites contamination by harmful bacteria.

If you must test for clarity, get fifteen inches of glass tubing from your local chemist (about ninepence), sterilize it and insert it into the jar. Keeping it upright, lower it to the bottom. Place your thumb firmly over the end and, with thumb pressed in place, withdraw the tube. This will contain a sample of your wine from top to bottom of the jar. Having carried out the test, return the tube full of wine – keeping your thumb in place – and when the tube touches the bottom, take away your thumb and withdraw the tube. In this way there is no disturbance of the lees.

If the wine is clear, then bottle it; if not, leave it to clear.

Dryness

After fourteen days' fermentation in the fermenting vessel, when I put the wine into stone jars I found it rather dry. There is no suggestion of sourness and it is not vinegary; the dryness is quite pleasant. Will the fermentation that will go on for several more weeks use up the rest of the sugar so that the wine will be too dry when fermentation has finished altogether?

The wine is almost certain to be very dry – almost arid, as I once heard it described. If you feel that you would like a trace of this pleasant dryness to remain in the finished wine, then you need add only one pound of sugar per gallon, but if you would rather there were no traces of dryness, then it is best to add two pounds per gallon. Warm a quart of the wine, dissolve the sugar in it, and then add this to the bulk.

On the other hand, if you have two gallons of this wine, why not treat one gallon as I have suggested and then blend the two separate gallons at the time of bottling?

It should be borne in mind that much of the sugar added will be fermented out during the remainder of fermentation, so that the wine treated will not be too sweet.

Tea in Wine

In your recipe for 'Scotch Bravery' you add one dessert-spoonful of tea to a gallon of wine: surely this is too small a quantity to make itself felt?

Tea is a source of tannin, and tannin adds flavour to certain wines – especially to 'Scotch Bravery'.

Now, in the normal way, I do not recommend the addition of tannin to wines, for not only is there the matter of personal taste to be considered, but in the normal way sufficient tannin is given to the wine by the soaking and crushing of the fruit prior to fermentation. Too much tannin in a wine may give it the unmistakable flavour of strong tea. This may merely underlie the flavour, giving the wine a pleasant tang, or it may be so strong as to make one think that the wine is sour.

My recipes produce wines suitable for the average palate, and certainly I have had no complaints. However, all tastes are not the same and all must be considered. Red wines such as those produced by black grapes, blackcurrants, red plums and elderberries, for instance, usually contain sufficient natural tannin; this is absorbed by the wine during the soaking period.

The tannin is contained in the skins and pips, so that, if the pips are accidentally crushed, the wine might contain too much tannin and thus have the flavour I mentioned above.

White wines – those made from green grapes, yellow plums, greengages, in fact all wines which are not red – are usually deficient in tannin, but hardly anybody seems to notice it.

The recipe for 'Scotch Bravery' resulted from an experiment in which I wanted to use a tannin-bearing fresh fruit which was not available. Instead, I used raisins for the fruit and added the tea to make up for the tannin that would have been in the fresh fruit.

Readers with experience in making rhubarb and other white wines may wish to experiment by adding up to half a cupful of strongly made fresh tea to each gallon.

Drying the Bottles

I sterilized my bottles with sulphur-dioxide solution as you advised and then rinsed them in boiled water. I quickly got used to the whiff of gas, but I have a terrible job getting the bottles dry. This takes ages in an oven, for I find that the water condenses and remains a long time. I have used my hairdrier, but without much success. Can you suggest a quicker way of getting them dry?

I recommend the use of sulphur-dioxide solution to save you this trouble in getting the bottles dry.

The bottles are ready for use as soon as they have been rinsed with the boiled water. It is best, of course, if they are allowed to drain upside down for a few minutes.

Over-Vigorous Fermentation

When I bottled my wine after fourteen days' fermentation and covered the bottles as you told me, all the yeast rose to the tops of the bottles and is at present clogging the necks. Smaller pieces are rising and falling and the wine is fermenting very, very fast. Can you tell me what I can do to make the yeast settle, and do you think any harm will come of what is happening?

No harm will come to your wine, and I do not think you will be successful in attempts to make the yeast settle.

This has been caused by disturbing a vigorous ferment. It is nothing to worry about. As soon as fermentation eases up, the heavy particles of yeast will settle, but some will cling to the necks of the bottles. All you need to do is to leave things as they are for the time being, and when the yeast has settled, clean the necks of the bottles with a piece of cloth wrapped round the handle of a teaspoon. Dip this in boiling water before using it.

Isinglass

My plum brandy, made with plums and wheat, tasted really nice when I put it into jars after fourteen days' fermentation – even though it was not nearly clear and fermentation was still going on quite hard.

When it stopped fermenting it tasted even better, but it was slow to clear, so I put a little isinglass into each bottle as I bottled it. It is really beautifully clear now, but it does not taste nearly as nice as it did before I used the isinglass. I thought that if I used isinglass to get rid of the impurities the wine would taste even better.

Isinglass certainly deposited the impurities as you wished it to, but it also took down some of the tannin and probably some acid as well. If you try to rectify matters now you will probably spoil it further. Next time, add a little strong tea – about half a cupful – before using the isinglass.

The little tannin you add in this manner will make up for that taken down by the isinglass. This is my reason for advising the use of isinglass only as a last resort.

Clearing Parsnip Wine

I made some parsnip wine last March with parsnips I keep specially for wine-making, but it was not clear by Christmas – though it was quite nice to drink.

I boiled the parsnips for twenty minutes in one gallon of water, and ended up with only three and a half bottles of wine, when I had taken it off the heavy lees. I tried clearing the last two bottles by whipping a little egg-white into some of the wine and adding this to the bottles, but this seemed to make things worse. I then tried isinglass and that has made it worse than ever. I don't think we will be able to drink the rest.

Is there anything I can do to get these last two bottles clear?

I am afraid you boiled the parsnips too long and most likely you did not take off the scum that rose whilst boiling.

In future, if you use the recipes on pages 22 and 23, you will have no further trouble of this sort. As for clearing the remaining bottles you have, you could try filtering through boiled silver sand, but even if this does clear the wine it will not improve the flavour.

Since only two bottles are involved it might be best to add them to that expensive account labelled 'experience' and vow never to have this trouble again.

Natural Fermentation

Most of the recipes I am using advise the use of cloves or ginger and they say, 'Soak the fruit for seven days or until fermentation begins. When this happens, strain the fruit and let the fermentation go on until it is finished. Then bottle the wine.' There is no mention of adding the yeast.

I do not like the flavour of cloves, except in stewed apples, and I am not very fond of ginger; if I leave out the ginger and cloves in the recipes and then make the wine as the recipe says, do you think it will be all right?

Frankly, I do not think the wine will be much good. To allow a fruit-and-water mixture to begin fermenting, and to allow that ferment to make the wine, is a very unsatisfactory method, for I have found that in nine cases out of ten the wine turns sour long before it is ready to drink. In fact, the ferment you are allowing to make the wine might well be a souring ferment.

This obviously has occurred to whoever gave you the recipe, and the cloves and ginger are, most likely, included for the purpose of obliterating that sourness.

Use the recipes and directions that I am enclosing and note that there is no mention of spices of any kind.

Corking Too Soon

My wine in gallon glass bottles (carboys, I think you call them), was brilliantly clear, fermentation having ceased three months earlier. When I began to siphon it into bottles, the lees rose up into the wine, which seemed to start working again. It stopped after about ten minutes, but I am afraid to bottle it in case it starts working again in the bottles and explodes them. I am leaving it covered with cotton-wool as you advised, and will do nothing until I have heard from you. Will you please hurry your reply?

PS. The wine is clearing rapidly again and tastes delicious. Do you think it will be all right?

Carboys they are. Your postscript confirms that bacteria are not responsible for the trouble and that your wine will be quite all right if you cork it hard now and bottle again when it has cleared.

Probably what happened is that you corked the carboys just a little too soon and accidentally produced a semi-sparkling wine. It is a wonder the bung didn't blow out of the carboy.

There is no fear of this happening again with this brew as you have allowed all the captured (compressed) carbon-dioxide gas to escape. So go ahead with bottling as soon as the wine is clear again, and don't forget to seal the bottles.

Campden Tablets

Could you tell me the minimum number of Campden tablets that will effectively preserve my wines? I am so afraid of getting some of that pungent sulphur smell in the finished wine.

During recent experiments to find the absolute minimum number of Campden tablets that will hold undesirable ferments in check while allowing the yeast to ferment the must satisfactorily, it was found that only one Campden tablet per gallon was needed when the fruit had been gathered fresh from the garden. One and a half to two were needed when the fruit was bought at a shop and so was, quite naturally, less fresh and not in such good condition.

Similar experiments revealed that as many as three tablets could be added to a well-flavoured wine without there being a trace of sulphite flavour in the finished wine.

If you find that there does happen to be a slight flavour of the sulphite in a finished wine, aeration by decanting will put matters right.

Reclaiming the Yeast

I have been using the Respora yeast you recommended. A week ago I had some fruit given me and decided to make wine with it. I had everything ready for adding the yeast and discovered that I had no yeast starter ready; worse still, I had no yeast in the house. However, I siphoned a little of the yeast deposit from a jar of fermenting wine and added this to the prepared must. This is now fermenting well, but I am wondering if everything will be all right.

Everything will be all right. This is a practice often resorted to. However, the yeast deposit from a jar that has finished fermenting should not be used, as the alcohol formed in the wine would most likely have destroyed the yeast organisms, so that all you would be putting into the must in this event would be dead yeast cells.

Cloudiness

Six bottles of gooseberry wine that I bottled recently have cleared nicely, but for a layer of cloudiness at the top of each bottle. How can I get rid of this?

If rocking the bottles from side to side has no effect, it is best to put a funnel into the top of each bottle – very gently – and then to pour in a little wine; this will overflow this 'top sediment' out of the bottles.

This is better than trying to get it to settle, which is rarely successful.

Fermentation Locks

I have some blackberry port fermenting under a fermentation lock. It has been fermenting slowly for some time (I used a port yeast), but now the water in the trap remains pushed up on one side, and nothing seems to be happening. Would you say that fermentation has ceased?

This is a little problem that those new to fermentation locks are likely to run up against. Fermentation *may* have finished, in which event the water will return to normal later on; but this may take from only a few days to a fortnight. Best plan is to keep the jar in a warm place, and then, when the water returns to normal, you can be fairly sure that fermentation has ceased.

On the other hand, fermentation may only have 'stuck', and in a few days may be on the go again quite merrily. Provided you are in no hurry to put the lock to further use elsewhere, I'd leave it a month longer if I were you.

An alternative would be to remove the lock and bung and to sample the merest drop; if this seems a little too sweet, it is reasonably safe to say that the yeast needs to be got going again. The best thing to do is to transfer the wine to another jar and to refit the lock. The airing given will most likely get fermentation on the go again.

If you have not a spare jar, insert a piece of sterilized glass or polythene tubing and give a gentle blow (I can hear the purists denouncing me for this), to aerate the wine. If there is no suggestion of acidity when you sample it, give it another nutrient tablet, fit the lock again and keep the jar in a warm place for a month. Fermentation will most likely get going again; if nothing happens within two weeks, then you can be certain that fermentation is finished.

22

Grow Your Own Wine

If you have a garden – or even if you have only a tiny plot of trampled-down, weed-infested soil – you can grow the fruits to make your own wine.

A plot measuring twelve feet by twelve will support three blackcurrant bushes and two gooseberry bushes, or two of each and two redcurrant bushes or some loganberry or raspberry canes. A plot twice that size or, say, thirty feet by twenty, which is really quite small, has enormous possibilities for growing each of the fruits just mentioned, and in addition rhubarb in quite large quantities.

I shall always remember a family who live just off the Holloway Road, London; they had a small garden with a few flowers in it, the main strip being grass, and pretty poor grass at that. Today they grow redcurrants, loganberries, raspberries, blackcurrants, rhubarb and grapes. The wines they make with these fruits they serve with meals or sip as they watch television at the comfort of their own fireside. They also have an elderberry tree which I gave them as a cutting. From this they make twenty-six or more bottles of wine a year. From the other fruits they make between thirty and fifty bottles of wine each season according to the weight of their crops. Their worst year produced fifty-seven bottles, their best year eighty-nine bottles – all at practically no cost at all and with precious little equipment. As for the time spent in making the wine – just an hour or so when the crops were ripe.

There are countless thousands of tiny plots of soil

like theirs throughout London and its suburbs alone; how many more there are in seaside towns and industrial areas is anybody's guess – there must be millions. And whatever their conditions right now, all could very easily be turned into 'vineyards'. Some may be closed in by high walls and fences, but this does not matter provided they get a few hours' sunshine on those rare days when the sun does happen to show itself.

Your fruits may not be of show quality, but this does not matter either. I have made first-class ports and burgundies from fruits grown under what experts would call impossible conditions.

The advantages of home-grown fruits cannot be over-emphasized. Not only are we able to prepare for making the wine at the right time, but we are also able to estimate the amount of fruit we shall have available. Apart from this, our fruit will be in the best possible condition for the job in hand and it will have cost us practically nothing.

Last summer, a friend of mine made two gallons of blackcurrant wine. He bought the currants at a shop and they were pretty badly bashed about by the time he got them home. Together with the sugar the wine cost him about 22*s.* per gallon – or about 4*s.* 6*d.* a bottle. My ports and burgundies cost me about 4*s.* 6*d.* a gallon – or about 11*d.* a bottle.

But apart from these very important points, my fruit was fresh, clean and free from the germs and dirt normally picked up during marketing, which, as we have seen, cause a lot of trouble during the making of the wine.

The varieties of fruits listed are not necessarily the latest, but rather those that have stood the test of time and come through with flying colours.

If, when you have gathered the fruit, you find you have not enough to make the amount of wine you had planned, do not let this prevent you getting under way.

You can always begin with a pound or so less than the recipe calls for and add more to the fermenting must a few days later when a second picking is possible. So that mistakes do not occur, begin with the right amount of water and label the fermenting vessel 'Add another pound of fruit', or whatever quantity is needed to make up the full amount. And if it so happens that you haven't enough of one kind of fruit to make as much wine as you want, do not let this bother you either, for there are recipes in this book that allow for a mixture of fruits.

Certain fruits are more suitable for making certain types of wine than others are. It is as hopeless to try to make port from gooseberries as it would be to try to grow apples on a plum tree. Therefore we must use blackcurrants, plums, elderberries and such-like for ports and burgundies, and the lighter-coloured fruits such as pears, raspberries, red- and whitecurrants and white grapes for light table wines, both sweet and dry, and dessert wines. Rhubarb and gooseberries are very suitable for making into champagne-style wines, and ripe gooseberries – those that have been left on the bushes to turn red or yellow according to variety – will make good imitations of sherry.

Manures and leaves and so on are out of the question for townspeople, so the first step for those who cannot get anything of this sort is to build up a supply of humus ready for digging in either at the time of digging the plot or when the trees or bushes are planted. Even those able to obtain small amounts of manure and leaves should save everything they can for the compost pit. Chemical fertilizers play an important part in modern gardening, but these cannot put into the soil the organic matter it needs if it is to remain healthy.

Worms – the invisible assets of the garden – do inestimable good below the surface of the soil, but they need something to live on. And remember that a soil without worms is poor and unhealthy.

Compost, apart from encouraging the activity of worms, gives the plants the organic matter they need, besides retaining moisture during dry spells. Regular digging-in of compost during spring will quickly change a poor soil to a good rich one capable of producing strong healthy growth and heavy crops. The little trouble taken in the early stages will repay you a hundred times over.

Dig a pit about three feet each way and three feet deep; if you have a few stones or bricks to line the bottom, so much the better, for this will assist drainage. A pit this size will be quite big enough for a small garden. Anything may be thrown into that pit: spent flowers from the house, all cabbage and potato peelings from the kitchen, tea-leaves, torn-up magazines and newspapers, straw, lawn mowings, leaves and spent flowers from other parts of the garden – in fact, anything and everything that will rot.

If any kind of manure is available – rabbit, poultry or stable manure – however small the amount, this too should go into the pit as it will help to rot down the other stuff. If you or your neighbour keep poultry, so that you have a regular supply of chicken manure, it is better to dry it out and keep it aside for hoeing in during the spring. Only put a very little of this manure round each plant, as it is very powerful and can do great harm. Just a dusting is enough. In its wet state it is far less potent. Cleanings from pigeon lofts, when dry, are even more potent than chicken manure, and should be used more sparingly still.

A valuable source of supply of compost matter is a friendly greengrocer willing to put aside cabbage trimmings for you. Remember that you cannot have too much of this stuff.

When you have a layer about four inches thick at the

bottom of your compost pit, sprinkle lime over the surface and then a two-inch layer of soil and tread it down. Then start again with a fresh layer of refuse and then more lime and soil and so on until the pit is full. Finish it off with a layer of earth and leave it until digging or planting time comes along. You haven't finished yet; start another pit so that when the first is used you will have another in the making. This will repay you well, I assure you.

Flock mattresses and such-like should be put aside for pulling to pieces and burying under the spot chosen for planting fruit bushes. Broken-up bones buried in the same fashion will fertilize the soil for years to come. Always try to have compost etc. available for mulching bushes in the spring. A mulch is merely a layer of compost, or leaves or lawn-mowings spread round and underneath the bushes and along rows of raspberry canes or loganberries. This helps to keep the roots cool during hot weather and helps to conserve moisture, besides fertilizing the fine hairy roots near the surface. The mulch is usually forked into the surface during late summer or early autumn.

Fair results will be obtained without a great deal of after-attention, but for the best results we must not only prepare our soil well but also take that little after-care that makes so much difference to the size and quality of our crops – and therefore the amount and quality of the wines we make.

I have mentioned that I have made first-class ports and burgundies from fruits grown under what experts would call impossible conditions. The reader might well argue that skill in making the wine will make up for poorness of ingredients. This is not so, for I have seen top-quality fruits turned into most disappointing wines. Good-quality fruits and a reasonable amount of care in making the wine are all that is needed; and some good wines can even be made from quite poor fruits. But it would not be untrue to say that the quality and the amount of wine you will make later on will depend on the care you take in preparing the soil now.

Whatever the condition of your soil, it can be improved immensely by a thorough digging now and a little attention from time to time. If your garden is already cultivated, you are more than halfway there; and if you are already growing fruits you are nine-tenths of the way to drinking those finished ports, burgundies and such-like.

On the other hand, if your plot – like so many others – is trampled down and apparently useless, you will have to start from scratch. However, immense satisfaction – pride, even – will be yours when those bottles of wine are ready to drink and when you recall that it wasn't so long ago when you were rather ashamed of that patch of ground you had been intending to dig up for years.

Starting from scratch has many advantages, too; it allows you to plan the layout without worrying about Auntie's London Pride or that azalea Grandad put in and which never does flower anyway, but which is sacred to the whole family simply because Grandad put it there.

The first step with an uncultivated plot is, of course, to dig it. Dig deeply and incorporate any leaves or compost you happen to have and, when you have finished, spread a little lime over the surface.

A month later, rake this in and dress the whole plot with bonemeal at the rate of a quarter-pound per square yard. Then fork this in lightly and leave the plot to the elements. Rain, frost, snow, wind and sunshine all put something into the soil; it is best then if the first digging is done in late summer or early autumn so that the soil is ready for late winter planting.

Considering Possibilities

The method of growing each fruit is described separately under the appropriate heading, but here it is as well to consider possibilities.

If you have a wall or wooden fence facing south your luck is in – provided it gets a bit of sunshine each day. Grapes, raspberries and loganberries can be grown against it. If a wall or fence is not available these three fruits may be grown on wires stretched across the garden, taking up practically no room at all.

Vertical stakes at four-foot intervals (six foot if they are concrete) embedded in the soil along a path or across the garden may be connected by strong wires and the trees, vines or canes tied in against them.

The first wire should be eighteen inches above the soil and subsequent wires two feet above each other. The stakes should project six feet above the soil.

The same principle is applied to a wall or fence. Fruits grown in this fashion leave room for other fruits such as blackcurrants and gooseberries. When planting remember that all fruits like sunshine; do not plant tall stuff so that it takes the sun from the shorter bushes and low-growing fruits such as strawberries and rhubarb.

Liquid Manures

There are many ways of making these valuable feeding materials; probably the easiest of all is to obtain a proprietary brand and follow the directions on the bottle.

Alternatively, if small amounts of stable or farmyard manures are available and also a tank, it is a good plan to soak the manure in water for a few days and then pour off the water and dilute this to the colour of straw before feeding it to the bushes and canes. This will also help to rot down compost if a little is sprayed, or sprinkled from a watering-can, over the top of the pit.

This should never be used stronger than advised, though it can be used in some strength on the compost heap. If fed to the plants when insufficiently diluted it may burn the roots. Never feed the bushes or canes when the soil is dry. Wait for an evening's rain or a heavy shower, and wait for rain to soak into the soil before you feed them.

If you cannot wait for rain, soak the ground well with a hose and feed a few hours later. If you happen to live near a friendly farmer he may be willing to let you have a gallon of the drainings from the manure heap occasionally. This is very strong and must be diluted to the colour of light straw before using.

Regular applications of compost and feeding with liquid manure is every bit as good as annual dung spreading.

Chemical Fertilizers

At Rothamsted, Hertfordshire, in 1843, John Bennet Lawes founded the first agricultural research station in the world. He and his assistant, Gilbert, experimented to find out exactly what plants needed to make them grow; and it may be said that together they laid the foundations upon which has been built our present-day agricultural knowledge.

It is surprising that in this age of enlightenment there are people who will put up with poor crops rather than use chemical fertilizers. They cannot be convinced that chemical fertilizers merely add to the soil what would ordinarily be there if they dunged their land each year.

In the good old days a load of farmyard manure was delivered for next to nothing to anybody who wanted it. But there are many more gardens these days and much less manure. Plants cannot take up solids; thus, whatever is dug into the soil must become liquid before the plants can use it. Solid manures in any form – scrap leather, wool-shoddy, fish waste, dung, etc. – take a long time to become available to the plants. And the only difference between natural manures and chemical fertilizers is that one is produced naturally, the other artificially.

Chemical fertilizers, especially in liquid form, are taken up by the plants almost at once, for science has merely put into bottles and packets what would ordinarily be delivered by the farm cart. These bottled and packeted stuffs carry directions which prevent over- or under-feeding, and ensure heavy healthy crops. Compost and other waste matter dug into the soil have the same moisture-retaining properties as farmyard manure: feeding with chemical fertilizers merely makes up the deficiency.

That, broadly speaking, is all there is to it; but make no mistake about it, a great debt is owed by mankind to John Bennet Lawes.

23

Growing Soft Fruits

GOOSEBERRIES

Gooseberries do quite well anywhere, but they do better on an 'open' soil, by which I mean fairly gritty. Therefore it will pay to dig in some moisture-holding material such as compost and, if possible, some gravel or shingle if the soil is inclined to be heavy. A light, sandy soil will need only the addition of compost.

A generous mulch during the early growing season will be of special benefit, as will fortnightly feeding with liquid manure. Plant any time between the beginning of October and mid-March. During a warm spell in February is the latest I, myself, would leave the planting of gooseberries.

Take out a hole to the depth of twelve or fifteen inches and about two feet across and put in a four-inch layer of compost and a shovelful of lightening material if the soil is heavy.

Spread out the roots and shovel sifted soil over them in four-inch layers. Tread each layer, but do not put more than your normal weight on it. A little compost may be mixed with the top soil if you have enough of it.

When all the soil has been returned, tread it firm but do not be tempted to stamp. The need for firm planting cannot be over-emphasized as the death of young trees and bushes is usually traceable to insecure planting.

The best results are obtained from a sunny position, but gooseberries do well in the shade provided they get *some* direct sunshine. The more sun they get the better will be their colour and flavour.

For wine-making, gooseberries are usually picked unripe, while they still retain that tartness that makes us screw up our eyes; this tartness is not found in the finished wine.

Pruning

Many people neglect this important task in the belief that the bigger the bush the bigger the crop. The opposite is the truth. An overgrown bush appears to produce more fruit – in fact it produces an abundance of inferior crop. Weight for weight, a well-groomed bush will produce nearly twice as much as a neglected one.

Pruning must be done with the idea of keeping the bush as open as possible in the middle; this will allow sun and air to get to the fruit. Fruit is produced on one-year-old wood; the whole idea then must be to cut back old growths so that the bushes produce plenty of new wood. Note the growths that have borne fruit and cut these back so that the wood produced whilst the fruit was growing is left to bear the next year's crop.

Prune back to a bud pointing away from the middle of the bush and prune in October or November.

Varieties (Reds): LORD DERBY has a good flavour; LANCASHIRE LAD is a favourite with the trade and is a good all-round variety; WHINHAM'S INDUSTRY is the best-flavoured red, and does quite well in the shade.

Whites: WHITESMITH is a vigorous grower which crops heavily and has a very good flavour – probably the best white.

Greens: LANGLEY GAGE, small fruits of excellent flavour. LANCER is a late variety, one of the best all-round sorts with a very good flavour. KEEPSAKE is a well-flavoured large fruit.

Yellows: LEVELLER is the heaviest cropping yellow – quite one of the best; GOLDEN DROP is a good one if you like sweet gooseberries. This variety is rather subject to attacks by mildew. Greens are best for wine-making, though many people like the wines made from yellows and whites. The reds often make a good imitation of sherry.

American gooseberry mildew may not attack the bushes at all, but if it does it usually appears in May. It is a grey-white cobweb-like film that clings to the leaves and fruits. Later it becomes 'mealy' and spreads to other bushes. Another type covers the fruit and young shoots with a felt-like, brownish substance. If these troubles arise, make up a wash consisting of three-quarters of a pound of washing soda, half a pound of soft soap and five gallons of water. Spray the bushes with this at 10- to 12-day intervals, beginning when the fruits have set. Three sprayings should be enough.

Gooseberry and Currant Sawfly may make their appearance and lay eggs from which small green caterpillars emerge. These eat the leaves so rapidly that if they are not controlled they may completely defoliate the bushes. The result is that the fruit drops off and growth of new wood is halted.

Much can be done by looking to the undersides of the leaves as soon as they are fully open; any with clutches of yellow eggs on them should be pinched off and burnt.

Poison washes should be used with care owing to the risk of poisoning the fruit. Spraying with derris is most effective if carried out early.

Greenfly sometimes attacks gooseberry bushes; a reliable brand of aphicide sprayed on the bushes will soon take care of them.

BLACKBERRIES

There are many Continental and British varieties of blackberry in cultivation in this country – and all make wine to suit various tastes. But the best blackberry port and burgundy is made from the wild blackberry gathered from the hedgerows of the countryside. If you have a bit of ground to spare at the end of the garden – say six feet wide and running the width of the garden – there is ample room for wild blackberries to grow well and produce several pickings of these delicious fruits each season.

Blackberry bushes crop up in the oddest places, and all those interested should be on the look-out for them on derelict building sites and waste ground, etc. Carefully lifted in late summer or early autumn – or early winter if the fruiting season has been late – they may be transplanted with ease.

If they happen to be bulky and difficult to carry off, cut them back ruthlessly and bring away the roots with a few three- or four-inch stems attached.

Wild blackberries will grow anywhere and require no attention apart from occasional thinning out of old wood and the shortening of long growths so that they do not take up more space than can be spared for them. A trip to the countryside during late September will enable you to find all the plants you want – you need only two, or three at the most.

The soil beneath them need not be kept clear of grass; indeed, I have picked the best blackberries ever from the edges of fields where the grass grew to the height of two feet and more. Wild blackberries will ripen sooner or later without much sun.

Cultivated Varieties. HIMALAYAN GIANT crops heavily and has a good flavour.

EDWARD LANGLEY crops early and well and also has a good flavour.

The PARSLEY-LEAVED or CUT-LEAVED varieties crop well with large shiny fruits of good flavour.

Cultivated blackberries must be grown in the same fashion as loganberries and like a similar soil.

Like loganberries, they are singularly free of any serious pests and diseases, though they are sometimes attacked by the maggot of the Raspberry Beetle (see Raspberries, p. 200).

LOGANBERRIES

Named after the American Judge Logan, who is the first recorded as having raised the fruit as we know it today. Loganberries must be trained along wires against a wall or fence or in the open garden. A sunny position is best, of course, but they do quite well with a few hours' sunshine each day provided they are not allowed to become overcrowded. Pinching off a few leaves so that the fruits are exposed to light and air will assist ripening if we do this when the fruits are of good size and nearing maturity.

Fruit is produced on the canes grown the previous years; therefore the canes that have borne fruit are cut down to within an inch of the soil in the autumn and the canes that have been growing up throughout the season are tied in against the wires.

PLANTING

Plant before Christmas if possible, but in any case not later than a mild spell in February. Take out the soil to a depth of twelve to fifteen inches and about two feet across. Put in a generous layer of compost, or rotted manure if this is available. Return some of the soil and firm this by gentle treading. Rest the plant on this and carefully spread fine soil over the roots; lift the plant up and down to allow the soil to filter between the roots. Firm each layer by gentle treading. Tie in the canes firmly at planting time.

A mulch during April and May will help towards a heavy crop and strong new growth.

Loganberries are usually free from any serious pest or diseases, but they are sometimes attacked by the maggot of the Raspberry Beetle (see Raspberries, p. 200).

BLACKCURRANTS

The best blackcurrants are those grown under ideal conditions, of course; but I have made excellent 'ports' and burgundies from fruits far below top quality.

Blackcurrants like a sunny position and a soil containing plenty of humus. If manure is available so much the better; if not, use compost.

Dig a hole wide and deep enough to accommodate all the roots. Put in a generous layer of compost or manure and then return about six inches of the soil. Firm this by treading, then stand the bush upon this and spread out the roots. Return the soil a little at a time and tread each layer to firm the roots.

A mulch of manure or compost in the spring, and generous feeding throughout the growing season, will help enormously towards a heavy crop and strong, healthy growth for subsequent years' fruiting. The bushes should be allowed four feet each way.

Plant between November and March. A mild spell in February is the latest that I myself would leave the planting of blackcurrants.

Pruning is usually carried out in the autumn, but usually I prune my bushes as soon as the fruit have been gathered and again in the spring if there is any suggestion of the bushes becoming overcrowded in the centre. Fruit bushes are rarely kept sufficiently 'open' in the centre. Pruning should be carried out with this idea in mind and also to make the bush produce as much new wood as possible.

Fruit is produced on wood that grows whilst the bush is developing fruit – that is, the wood grown this year will bear next year's fruit. Our aim then must be to cut out the wood that has borne fruit, leaving the wood that grew during the season to bear next year's fruit. New growth is easy to detect, and the beginner will be able to decide which pieces to cut out and which to leave.

Always cut back to a bud, and cut clean. If you happen to damage a bud, cut back to the next one and be more careful this time. This sort of damage may result in the whole branch dying back.

Look to the bushes during winter; if you notice that some of the buds are swollen and rounded instead of being the same shape and size as the rest of them, pinch them off and burn them. This is known as *Big-Bud*. The buds are swollen by the mites inside them. When the buds open in spring the mites emerge and do irreparable damage; the leaves are eaten and the crop is small.

It is best to spray the bushes with a proprietary brand of insecticide as soon as the leaves are open and again a week later.

Varieties. Good all-round varieties that crop well and make good wines are BOSKOOP GIANT, SEABROOK'S BLACK, and SEPTEMBER BLACK.

RED- AND WHITECURRANTS

Preparation of the soil, the most suitable position, and the distance between bushes are the same as for blackcurrants. But whereas with blackcurrants we prune with the idea of making the bushes produce as much new wood as possible, the pruning of red and whitecurrants is aimed at achieving almost the reverse.

The best plan is to encourage these bushes to produce seven or eight main branches. The new, lateral growths – those growing outwards from the main branches – are cut back during the autumn so as to leave four or five buds on each.

Strong new branches growing from the trunk should be encouraged so that older main branches can be cut out when they get a bit too old. If new branches have formed there will be no loss of productivity. The leaders, or main branches (those bearing the laterals) should be cut back by from one-third to one-half in the autumn.

Always make a clean cut back to a bud growing away from the centre of the bush. Cut out dead wood.

Pruning should not be delayed later than late October.

Red- and Whitecurrants are sometimes subject to the same pests and diseases as blackcurrants.

Varieties: The best white is WHITE VERSAILLAISE. DUTCH RED is an excellent red which crops regularly and heavily. The variety I grow myself is LAXTON'S NO. 1, the best redcurrant of all. It may be relied upon to grow freely and crop heavily each season with quite enormous bunches of fruits of good colour and flavour, and the individual fruits are large.

RASPBERRIES

Raspberries will do well almost anywhere provided the soil is prepared well and they get a little sunshine from time to time. They do quite well close to tall trees. Raspberries must be grown against wires attached to stakes at both ends of the rows. If the row is a long one the stakes should be set at six-foot intervals. This will

GROWING SOFT FRUITS

prevent sagging and possible damage to the canes. Raspberries may also be grown against a wall or fence that gets some sun.

It is best to dig a trench about fifteen inches deep and wide and into this put a generous layer of compost or manure. Return all the soil and firm by gentle treading.

If large clumps of roots are being put in, take out a hole deep enough and large enough all round to accommodate all the roots.

Plant carefully, spreading out the roots. Return the soil a little at a time and firm each layer by gentle treading.

Plant these large clumps about eighteen inches to two feet apart.

If one-year-old canes are being planted, put them in groups of three at nine-inch intervals. They may be put in singly at nine-inch intervals, but they seem to do better in groups.

Tie the canes to wires, and in the autumn following the fruiting season cut down the canes that have fruited, and tie in those that have been growing up throughout the season. The old canes should be cut down to within three inches of the soil.

Any new canes that look at all puny compared with the others are best cut down, leaving only the strongest half-dozen canes from each clump to produce next season's fruit.

This may seem wasteful, but it is not, for much better fruits will be produced on the stronger canes.

A mulch of manure or compost in the spring will help enormously in producing a heavy crop and in making healthy new canes to bear the subsequent season's fruit.

Varieties: PARK LANE is probably the best-flavoured variety, but is rather soft and therefore rather too easily damaged during gathering. HAILSHAM is a deep-coloured, vigorous grower with a good flavour. ROYAL is a very large fruit of excellent flavour. LLOYD GEORGE is both very fertile and very vigorous. This variety may be cut to within three inches of the soil in the spring and will fruit in the autumn on the canes made during the season. Conditions for success in this treatment must be near ideal – that is, plenty of manure or compost and a sunny position. Otherwise this raspberry, probably the best of the lot – may be treated as those above.

Maggots of the Raspberry Beetle sometimes make their appearance in spring. The beetle lays eggs which hatch into maggots that eat into the berries. The beetles are very small, about one-fifth of an inch long, and usually golden in colour, but are sometimes a muddy grey. The maggots are about a quarter-inch long and creamy-white. The best method of control is to keep a look-out for the beetle and to spray with derris if you spot any.

STRAWBERRIES

With so many other fruits available for making wines, I cannot imagine anybody using home-grown strawberries for this purpose, except for the rare individual who does not like strawberries and cream. Strawberries are not difficult to grow, but sometimes they are a job to ripen properly – our summers being what they are. The soil for strawberries must be well prepared, with a liberal digging-in of compost or manure.

August is the best time for planting, for this allows the young crowns to become established in time for the fruiting season next year. If the weather happens to be very dry at planting time, they will need a good soaking with water every evening until they are established – or until rain comes.

Plant the young crowns very carefully, being sure

that the crowns are neither higher nor lower than the surface of the surrounding soil and that the roots are well spread out. Plant the crowns eighteen inches apart in rows about two feet apart.

Strawberries need a dressing of manure as soon as the flowers have set. Later, as the fruits begin to swell, clean straw should be spread round the plants to keep the fruits clean. Strawberry mats may be obtained from seedsmen for this purpose, but they can prove an expensive outlay. As runners form, pinch them off and keep pinching them off until you need new plants.

When this time arrives, the first little crown growing on the runner is pegged down and the runner pinched off beyond this point. The best plan is to select the strongest runners from the plants bearing the heaviest crops and to pinch out all others. Those pegged down to form new plants may be severed from the runner later on to make a new bed.

Varieties: ROYAL SOVEREIGN is probably the best of the lot. Besides being a heavy cropper it is quite hardy, the fruits being large and of excellent flavour. SIR JOSEPH PAXTON is also hardy and prolific. This one fruits a bit later than Royal Sovereign; it has a good colour and flavour and does well on the heavier soils.

RHUBARB

Probably the easiest of all fruits to grow well. It will push up some sort of crop under the most adverse conditions and always seems able to produce a good flavour, regardless of soil and situation.

For the best results a little attention to the soil before planting is needed and this will repay you a thousand times over.

Much of my own rhubarb attains the height of up to thirty inches and is as thick as a man's wrist, but half these measurements could be regarded as average. I have paid little attention to my rhubarb since it became established years ago; I did, however, take care in preparing the soil.

In one abnormally dry spring, mine, like most other people's in the south, withered and died down completely. The wet summer brought it up again and I had one of the best crops for years, making ten gallons of wine with it, besides having plenty for use in the kitchen and for my wife to preserve two dozen two-pound bottles. The crowns appear not to have suffered, for there is still a splendid crop. You may one day experience this dying down, so do not worry.

Dig as deeply as you can. Two or even three feet is not too deep provided the sub-soil is not stony. If leaf-mould is available, fork in as much as you can spare. Manure should never be put underneath rhubarb, but a top-dress of manure in February will help towards a heavy crop. The best plan is to get half a dozen crowns – at about ninepence each – and plant in a single row at two-foot intervals. If more than one row is put in there should be at least a yard between them.

February is the best time for planting rhubarb, though it can be left until as late as the end of March. Plant the crown so that the red bud or 'button' is just showing above the soil. Plant firmly.

It is tempting to pull a few sticks during the first season, but this *must* be resisted if the crowns are to get a chance to establish themselves. Do not use any rhubarb during the first year.

If flower heads form – watch out for these during a dry spring or dry early summer – they should be broken off (not pulled up) at ground level. Clean up the bed in the autumn by picking up dead leaves and sticks and, if such is available, cover the bed with straw or bracken or dried fern from a common. This may be kept in place by a string tied to a couple of stakes at each end of the bed so that it pulls downwards – this will hold the litter down. This winter covering is not essential but the next year's crop will be earlier and all the better for this treatment.

Varieties: Both CHAMPAGNE and MYATT'S VICTORIA do well and there seems to be little to choose between them.

Needless to say, pruning is not necessary. Some advise splitting up the crowns after three years; I do not advise this. Some of the best rhubarb I have seen – see regularly each year, in fact – comes from beds that have not been touched for twenty years and more. And all the treatment these beds get is an annual top-dress of well-rotted manure and a hoeing during the early season to keep down weeds.

Forced rhubarb – those pretty, pink sticks with crinkled leaves – are not suitable for wine-making.

24

Growing Tree Fruits

APPLES

There are countless varieties of apples in general cultivation in this country and all have their likes and dislikes – yet all the all-round varieties seem to do well almost anywhere.

Like all fruits they like to be treated well and will reward those who remember this. I am concerned with growing apples and other fruits such as plums for winemaking; therefore there seems little point in covering the growing of these fruits in the espalier fashion or as cordons. Apart from the fact that the average homegrower will not want this type of tree, he will want as much fruit as he can get from as little space as he can allow. No one will dispute the quality of fruits grown as cordons, but they are expensive to start with and cannot hope to compete with the bush tree when a lot of fruit is the aim of the grower.

The bush tree is the most suitable for the small garden where the owner wants as much fruit as he can get from a small space and for a minimum of labour.

Deep digging is essential, for it must be remembered that trees, once planted, will remain perhaps the lifetime of the owner.

The roots of apples go a great deal deeper than is generally imagined and provided the right variety for the type of soil is planted, the trees will settle down and fruit well. Unless your garden is in what we call a 'frost hole' – a natural depression in the lie of the land that catches the spring frosts harder than elsewhere and then catches the first rays of the morning sun – you can grow apples without fear of the frosts depriving you of your crops.

Bush apples are usually planted ten to twelve feet apart and are put in before Christmas. Early February is the latest that I would leave this job.

Prepare the soil well in advance and allow it to settle before planting. Six months in advance is not too early to get the first digging done if the soil has never before been broken.

Planting. Take out holes a good bit larger than are required to accommodate all the roots without cramping. The depth of the hole will depend on the depth the young tree had been planted before it was delivered to you and this will be clearly marked on the young trunk.

Any roots damaged in transit should be cut off cleanly with a sharp knife.

It is best to drive a stake firmly into the middle of the hole and to tie the tree to this while planting. Spread out the roots, shovel sifted soil over them and firm each layer by treading. 'Rattle' the tree occasionally so that the soil is shaken down between the roots. Plant firmly; insecure planting is the most frequent cause of deaths among young trees. When firmly planted, untie the tree from the stake and bind the trunk with felt or some other material and bind this part to the stake. This will prevent chafing of the bark.

Pruning. A book this size could be written about the pruning of tree fruits and even then the subject would not be covered fully.

For general purposes it is best not to prune a young tree during the first season after planting, but pruning thereafter is of the greatest importance. Not only does it keep the tree in shape but it prevents overcrowding and ensures regular and heavy fruiting.

In the case of bush apples, each leading shoot – that is the growing tip of each main branch – is cut back by about six inches. The young growths growing off this main branch are laterals; these must not be allowed to become branches otherwise the tree will become overcrowded. These laterals are pruned back to leave four or five buds.

Varieties. The best all-round varieties are WORCESTER PEARMAIN, JAMES GRIEVE, CHARLES ROSS, ELLISON'S ORANGE, BEAUTY OF BATH and LADY SUDELEY.

The following precautions should be taken against pests and diseases. Spray during winter with a tar-distillate wash. Spray with a nicotine wash in spring, when the buds begin to open and again a week after the petals have fallen. Fix grease bands to the trunks.

PLUMS

As with apples, plums are best grown as bush fruits in a small garden. They may be grown against a wall or fence, but the crops, whilst usually being of better quality, are small compared with those from bush trees.

Plums do well in the same positions and soil as apples and are planted in the same way. But because they flower rather early, the young buds are sometimes damaged by spring frosts – especially if the very early spring has been unusually warm and the trees in consequence are rather advanced. If plum trees can be planted so that a building or a tall tree can protect them, so much the better.

The damage is caused not so much by the frost, but by the early morning sun catching the buds and, by thawing them out too quickly, rupturing them. If there is a building to the east of the plums this will take the first rays of the sun, and by the time the sun reaches the buds they will have thawed.

Varieties. The VICTORIA plum is without doubt the best all-round variety and should be grown in every garden. It crops regularly and heavily and is self-fertile; that is, it does not need another plum tree handy as a pollinator, as in the case of certain other fruits.

PERSHORE and THE CZAR are other good varieties that should be grown wherever there is space for them.

Spray with tar-oil wash in winter. In spring spray with derris wash when the leaves are about half-size.

DAMSONS

These make excellent wines; they are quite easy to grow, being for all intents and purposes regarded as plums.

PEARS

Pears are another fruit best grown as a bush in small gardens; but, as with apples and plums, they may be grown against a wall or fence. And here, as with apples and plums, the crops are of better quality but not nearly so heavy. With the same soil and conditions as apples (see p. 204), pears will give good results, though, like plums, they sometimes need a little protection according to situation.

Plant as for apples and allow them twelve feet each way.

Pruning is the same as for plums and apples.

Varieties. LAXTON'S SUPERB is a very good variety with quite large fruits of excellent flavour; COLMAR D'ELITE is somewhat smaller, but this one has a very good flavour and is very sweet; the BARTLETT pear used extensively by the canning industry is known as WILLIAMS BON CHRÉTIEN; LOUIS BONNE is an October variety which should be found a place in every garden for it does well almost anywhere.

CHERRIES

Cherries do not do well everywhere; they dislike both heavy clay soils and light gravel ones. They are best grown as standards, though they do well against walls in favourable conditions. Grown against a wall they are unlikely to give enough fruit to make more than a gallon of wine at a time, and it is doubtful, where a small garden is concerned, whether enough fruit would be produced at one time to make even one gallon.

Grown as standards they occupy far more space than the average small- to fair-sized garden has to spare for them. Apart from these points, cherries like a lot of sun and they like it early because they mature early.

Readers interested in growing cherries would be well advised to discuss the matter with their local nurseryman; he will be able to tell them whether it would be worth while.

PEACHES, APRICOTS, NECTARINES

Unfortunately, the only really satisfactory method of growing these fruits is against a wall or fence and trained in the 'fan' or espalier fashion, when, as with plums and apples, the yield is unlikely to make large quantities of wine. They need a wall facing south, and considerable care and after-attention.

In the very warmest districts peaches and apricots might do well as standards, but these need something like twenty-five feet each way – rather more than can be spared for them. In any case, something like specialist treatment is needed to get the best results; and since I am concerned with growing fruits for wine-making and with readers who want as much as they can get from a small space and for the minimum of labour, there seems little point in including the growing of these fruits.

ELDERBERRIES

Elderberries are, of course, wild fruit, but this does not mean that they will not grow in a garden. Some of the best elderberries I have seen were growing at the end of a cultivated plot that formed part of what was then my garden. They are not mine now, but I have only to walk a few yards to get all the elderberries I need – something like thirty pounds a year for the great amount of wine I make from them.

In my opinion, elderberries are the best wild fruit for wine-making, for they make excellent ports and burgundies and, in fact, can very easily be made to imitate the best and most expensive red wines. They have that richness of colour and strength of flavour that characterizes the wines they make. Regular tipplers of good ports and expensive clarets have been unable to tell the difference between these and my elderberry wines. A friend of mine delights his visitors with 'cherry brandy' – made with elderberries. This will show the reader what can be done with this lowly fruit.

I don't think you will get an elderberry tree from your nurseryman, but a friend in the country will be able to get one for you. Otherwise a trip to the outskirts of the town you live in – not necessarily to the countryside, but where there are a few trees or waste land during August or September – should enable you to spot an elderberry tree with its massive clusters of black berries. They grow almost anywhere: round gravel and sand pits, on derelict building sites, waste land, railway embankments, chalk-pits – they love chalk-pits – and of course at the edges of woods and streams and along country lanes.

Go out and find one for yourself; earmark it if it is earlier than the end of September, and then return. Dig round and find yourself a young shoot with a good rooting system attached to it and cart it off.

This may not be the same advice as a nurseryman would give you, but it works – I've done it several times.

If you can get two or three roots for making two or three trees so much the better. Plant them where they will get plenty of sun but not so that they shade other fruits needing sunshine. They benefit by being cut down to within a foot or so of the soil after several years, so if more than one is planted you can still cut one down and have fruit the following year. By the time the next one needs cutting down the other one will be ready to fruit.

A good plan is to plant them at the far end of the garden and plant blackberries under them. They grow well together – often being found like this in their wild state.

If you happen to approach a nurseryman for an elderberry tree, tell him that you want it for wine-making, there being certain varieties grown merely for ornament.

I have never known the wild elderberry to suffer from any disease and they seem to do well however severe the winter or poor the summer.

25

Growing Grapes

I think it quite safe to say that more has been written about the cultivation of grapes than has – or ever will be – written about any other fruit. This is not surprising, considering that the grape is probably the oldest of known fruits. Evidence that grapes have been grown here for centuries is found in certain parts of the country where careful inspection of sloping land shows remains of terraced vineyards.

Contrary to general belief grapes are quite easy to grow outdoors in this country and should be grown by the ordinary householder far more than they are. It is a mistake to believe that grapes need tropical weather to grow and ripen well; if this were so they could not be grown in Russia and Canada, where the vineyards are buried under snow each year. Even the vineyards of France are not harmed by an annual blanket of snow. Then why should they suffer here?

The abundance of advice offered by experts about growing grapes, and the recommendations they make, are more likely to deter the would-be grower of grapes than encourage him in this worthwhile hobby. In any case, the advice and recommendations of experts usually apply to tender vines needing specialist treatment – not the good all-round varieties that do well almost anywhere. Here the reader will find sufficient detail to enable him to get on with the job and to make a good show of it into the bargain. Surprisingly, grapes do not need loads of manures and fertilizers; they grow well on quite poor soils and need little after-attention.

The soil above the vine I once grew was covered with crazy paving, the only part exposed to sun and air being about a square yard where the vine had been planted years earlier. So you can see that lack of space is no excuse for not growing grapes. The roots will search out and find what they want; all we have to concern ourselves with is where to put the top-growth – the vine itself.

If one wall of your house faces south, south-west or even west, that problem is solved very easily. If you cannot plant the vine under that particular wall, plant it round the corner and train the vine round to the sunny side of the house. Grapes may be grown in the open garden in similar fashion to loganberries, or they may be trained over sheds, garages, out-houses and such-like.

Vines are not expensive – about ten shillings and sixpence is a decent price to pay for a vine (at the present time), and if two are planted, the yield for one guinea may be regarded as fantastic when considering the value of the wine that may be made for many years.

The best outdoor, general-purpose vine is undoubtedly BRANDT. This is a free-growing black that crops heavily and does well almost anywhere. Brandt is the vine for the amateur wherever he may be living, for it is very hardy and needs very little attention. It is the only variety I need concern myself with here.

Planting is best carried out in autumn and in any case before Christmas. If planting against a wall, take out a hole about two feet each way and plant so that the stem of the vine is about fifteen inches away from the wall itself. Dig deeply and work in any compost that may be available and some builders' rubble if you can get some. A dusting of lime forked in will be helpful. Spread out the roots well and plant as recommended for fruit trees.

Having planted the vine, spread a little manure above

the roots: this will not be necessary in subsequent seasons, but the vine will benefit from a mulch each spring if you can give it one.

Vines must not be allowed to fruit the first season; therefore they must be cut back to about four buds.

Having planted the vine and cut it back, we must decide how to train it to cover the wall. The best plan is to use special wall nails, run wires to and from these and train the vine to the wires.

The four long growths that come from the four buds you left when cutting back are stopped at the bud nearest the growing point. These four leaders are the basis from which the vine will be built up to cover the wall. If flower buds form during the first season, they should be nipped off so that the vine uses its energy producing wood for subsequent fruiting. First-season fruiting often permanently weakens a vine.

If no shed, wall or garage is available, a vine can be grown on the trellis system in the open garden. Concrete posts are best as these last indefinitely. Set them at six-foot intervals and protruding six feet above the soil; a system of wires may be arranged in the same fashion as that used for a wall. One of the best outdoor vines I have seen in recent years was grown on six eighteen-foot lengths of galvanized water piping. These were supported by three concrete clothes-posts – one each end and one in the middle. The vine had been planted against the middle one and stopped (cut back), at a bud three feet from the ground.

The side shoots that made rapid headway the first season were trained along the lower piping and tied in with strips of leather cut from old riding boots.

The following season, the new growth growing from the bud that had been left when the vine had been cut back at planting time was tied to the middle post and stopped when it reached the top. Side shoots growing from this were trained along the higher piping. When the side growths – laterals – reached the ends of the piping, these also were stopped. The process of filling in the framework was then carried out.

In three years a framework of six eighteen-foot pipes had been filled in and was bearing heavily. The first pipe had been fixed fifteen inches from the soil and subsequent pipes fifteen inches above each other.

It will be seen that, apart from the need for rather stronger supports, grapes are as easy to grow as loganberries. All that should be borne in mind is that vines should be trained to rise slightly or remain on the horizontal – never downwards. When pruning, remember that next year's fruit will be borne on the wood made this year. But we do not want masses of long, straggling growths hanging about all over the place, so during the summer it is best to cut some of them out. Those left to bear next year's fruit should be cut back to five or six buds in autumn or early winter. Only new growth should be cut during the summer; *never* cut old wood during summer – indeed old wood must never be cut after Christmas, as this can cause profuse bleeding which may be quite impossible to stop. By all means cut away some of the old growth to make way for new wood, but if this has not been done before Christmas leave it until the next winter.

Brandt ripens in September – or earlier if the summer has been good. This is especially advantageous because the weather is still warm enough for a satisfactory ferment when you come to make the wine. This is not so important to those who carry out their fermentation in the house, but where it has to be carried on in a shed or outhouse the warm weather is a great help.

26

Monthly Gardening Reminders

JANUARY

Little can be done this month, and much will depend on how much has been done in previous months. If the weather is mild the planting of fruit trees and bushes may be undertaken, but do this only if the weather appears likely to stay mild for a few days at least.

Look to blackcurrant bushes and remove any swollen buds and burn them.

Get in supplies of insecticides and fertilizers.

FEBRUARY

Make sure all trained fruits are tied to their supports securely, and give each a mulch of manure if there is plenty available. If only limited amounts of manure or compost are available keep these till later on. Loganberries and raspberries not already cut down should be attended to and the new canes tied in.

If the weather is mild a light forking of the top soil round fruit bushes and along rows of canes, followed by a dusting of lime, will do a lot of good. This will also unearth a few pests for the attention of birds.

All fruit trees and bushes should have been planted by now; if they have not, get them in before the end of the month.

March

Gooseberries and currants should be sprayed this month with paraffin emulsion to safeguard them against brown scale and red spider.

Watch blackcurrants for 'big bud' and pinch off any suspects and burn them. Care must be taken now because the buds may be at the point of opening.

Fork round bushes and canes as for February if this was not done last month.

April

Spray blackcurrants with a lime and sulphur wash where 'big bud' is suspected. Repeat if necessary.

The main activity in the garden now will be spreading compost or manure and keeping down weeds before they get a hold.

Any weak growths on fruit bushes may be cut out so as to leave the stronger growths to bear the fruit. This will also help the growth of new wood on which next year's fruit will be borne.

May

To keep strawberries clean put clean straw round the plants. Before doing this dress the bed with two ounces of superphosphate per square yard and hoe this in lightly.

Give all fruit a mulch of manure or compost, or dead leaves. Begin weekly feeding with liquid manure.

Watch all fruit for signs of pests and diseases and spray with proprietary brands of insecticide.

June

Gooseberries often need thinning at this time of the year. Do this so that the smaller fruits are left to develop fully.

Make wine with the thinnings.

If the weather is very dry, mulch fruit bushes with manure, compost, leaves, straw, lawn mowings or whatever is available. Mulching conserves moisture in the soil and helps the fruit to swell. This can increase the annual yield by as much as a third.

If green-fly appears spray with a proprietary brand of insecticide.

JULY

Fruit bushes and trees make rapid growth at this time of the year. If there is any suggestion of overcrowding, cut out some of this new growth, leaving the strongest to grow on.

Look to the vines; if there is an abundance of long straggling growths, cut some of them out, leaving those you will want for cutting back in the autumn.

Runners from strawberry plants may be pegged down to make new plants. Peg down the strongest young crown on the runners that come from the plants bearing the heaviest crop. Pinch off the runner an inch beyond the crown to be pegged down. If this is not done the runner will continue to run and develop new crowns; this will weaken the parent plant and will also produce an abundance of new weakling plants. If tree-fruit crops are heavy, thin to two or three fruits to each cluster. Far better to have three good fruits to each bunch than five or six under-sized ones.

AUGUST

Keep down weeds with the hoe. Gather apples and pears if ready and look to later varieties: thin these as necessary.

September

Loganberries and raspberries that have borne fruit may be cut down now and the new canes tied in.

Clean up round trees and bushes and burn all leaves if pests and diseases have been prevalent. The ash, if there is enough of it, should be stored for hoeing in round fruit bushes in the spring. Hoeing now will help to prevent weeds growing from seeds dropped earlier.

Pegged-down strawberry runners may be lifted now, severed from the parent plant and planted out. Strawberry beds need replacing every three years; it is a good plan then to replace a third of the bed each year with these new plants.

October

Clean up and burn all rubbish round fruit bushes and canes. If loganberries and raspberries have not yet been cut down and the new canes tied in, do this now.

Prune currants and gooseberry bushes.

Plant fruit bushes and early varieties of tree fruits.

November

All those jobs that you should have done during August, September and October must be done now.

December

Look to blackcurrants for 'big bud'; pinch off infected buds and burn them.

Plant and prune vines, fruit trees, bushes and canes.

Make sure that you are getting a good supply of compost ready for next year.

Index

Acetic bacteria 6
Acid content 160, 168–9
Ales and beers 78–81
Apple wine 55, 118
Apples, growing of 204–6
Apricot brandy 35
Apricot wine 54–5
Apricot, prune and
  sultana wine 67

Barley water 36
Beetroot wine 23, 151
Blackberries, growing
  of 194
Blackberry burgundy 108, 141
Blackberry port 107
Blackberry wine 58, 108, 109, 141
Blackcurrant wine 49, 110, 135–6
Blackcurrant and
  rhubarb appetizer 47–8, 134
Blackcurrants, growing
  of 196–7
Blending 84–5
Brewing 78–81

Campden tablets 89, 93, 96, 103
Canadian whisky 29
Carrot whisky 26–7
Carrot wine 151–2

Celery wine 24
'Champagne' 153–7
— apple 156
— blackcurrant 156
— green gooseberry 156
— pear 156
— rhubarb 155
Cherries, growing of 208
Cherry brandy 40–1
Cherry wine 54, 109
Cider 75–7
Clarity, testing for 172–3
Clearing 15–16, 176–7, 180
Clover wine 68
Cloves and ginger 177–8
Coltsfoot wine 69–70
Corking 79–80, 178
Crab-apple wine 48–9, 134–5
Currant wine 64, 145
Currant, sultana and
  prune wine 66, 148

Damson port 112–13, 137
Damson wine 51–2, 113
Damson and apple
  wine 56
Damson and prune
  burgundy 114
Dandelion wine 69
Date wine 66, 147
Date, prune and
  fig wine 67
Distilling 86–7

INDEX

'Don't Mind if I Do'
   port 31-2
Dorking whisky 29-30
Dried-apricot wine 65, 146
Dried hops 80-1
Drying the bottles 175
Dryness 173-4

Egg-flip 73
Elderberries, growing
   of 209-10
Elderberry brandy 39
Elderberry wine 44-6, 116-18, 130-2
Elderberry and damson
   wine 46, 113-14, 132
Elderberry and prune
   wine 46-7, 133
Elderberry and raisin
   wine 47, 133-4
Elderflower champagne
   (non-alcoholic) 71

Fermentation 13, 170, 175-6
Fermentation locks 92-5
Fig wine 67
Filtering 102

Ginger beer 73
Ginger wine 41, 42
Gooseberries, growing
   of 191-3
Gooseberry sherry 122
Gooseberry wine 121-2
Grape wine 49, 51, 125-8
Grape and elderberry
   wine 51, 136-7
Grapefruit wine 57
Grapes, growing of 211-14
Greengage wine 53

Hops 172
Hydrometer 161-5

Isinglass 13-14, 176

Jungle Juice, extra
   special fine old 27
— Super-special
   improved 27-8

Law and the wine-
   maker 80, 86-7
Lemon wine 56-7
Loganberries, growing
   of 195-6
Loganberry brandy 40
Loganberry wine 57, 120-1, 139-40

Malt 80-1
Mangold wine 21, 151
Mead 33-4
Mint julep 72
Mixed root wines 22-3
Mulberry brandy 38
Mulberry wine, 54, 139

Norah's Delight 28
Norah's Favourite 152

Orange brandy 32-3
Orange wine 59, 141-2
Orange and raisin wine 30

Parsley brandy 35
Parsnip wine 20, 21, 150
Peach brandy 32
Pear wine 58-9, 119
Pears, growing of 207
Pea-shuck wine 25
Pectin 9-10

INDEX

Plum brandy 36–7
Plum port 120
Plum wine 52–3, 119, 138–6
Plums, growing of 206–7
Potato wine 21, 151
Prune wine 65, 145–6
Punch 72

Quince wine 55–6

Rainwater 5–6
Raisin wine 64, 144–5
Raisin, prune and sultana wine 66, 147
Raspberries, growing of 198–200
Raspberry brandy 39
Raspberry wine 58, 114, 140
Raspberry and date wine 140
Redcurrant wine 53–4, 111
Redcurrants, growing of 197–8
Rhubarb, growing of 201–3
Rhubarb brandy 37, 38
Rhubarb wine 119–20
Rice wine 43
Runner bean wine 24

Scotch Bravery 31
Serving wines 18
Sherry 61–3
Sherry cobbler 73
Siphoning 18
Sparkling wines ('champagnes') 108–12
Specific gravity 161–5

Spiced apple wine 78
Sterilization 10–12, 79
Storage 17
Straining 4
Strawberries, growing of 200–1
Strawberry wine 49, 115
Sugar 4
Sugar-beet wine 22
Sugar content 158–9
Sugar wine 69–71
Sulphur dioxide (SO_2) 12, 89, 93, 96
See also Campden tablets

Tangerine special 59–60
Tangerine and orange special 142–3
Tasting while blending 84
Tea in wine 174–5
Tea wine 72–3

Westcott schnapps 29
Wheat and raisins, as flavouring 171–2
Wheat wine 30, 43
Whitecurrant wine 112
Whitecurrants, growing of 197–8
Whortleberry wine 52, 122–4, 137–8
Wild yeast 6–9
Wine fly 10
Wine yeasts 89, 97–9

Yeast, baker's 5
Yeast nutrient 101
Yeast starter 100